INTERPERSONAL
COMMUNICATION

INTERPERSONAL

JOHN C. CONDON, JR.

COMMUNICATION

MACMILLAN PUBLISHING CO., INC.

New York

COLLIER MACMILLAN PUBLISHERS

London

Macmillan Publishing Co., Inc.
866 Third Avenue, New York, New York 10022

Collier Macmillan Canada, Ltd.

Library of Congress Cataloging in Publication Data

Condon, John C
  Interpersonal communication.

  Bibliography: p.
  Includes index.
  1. Interpersonal communication.   I. Title.
BF637.C45C66   158'.2   76-11852
ISBN 0-02-324210-8

Printing: 1 2 3 4 5 6 7 8   Year: 7 8 9 0 1 2 3

*This book is dedicated to Karen and Ed and Frank and
Louise and Arthur and Sandy and Charlie and Brownie and
Roger and Michiko and Don and Alice and Miguel and
Lloyd and Joan and Noah and Ann and Bob and Joel and
Martin and Lee and Russ and Andrew and Donna and
people like that. . . .*

PREFACE

INTERPERSONAL COMMUNICATION and *the study of* interpersonal communication are different. Things would be simpler if we used terms that reflected that difference, but today there is no standardized vocabulary in this field. The student of language has it easier: he studies language, he is a linguist, and his field is linguistics. A good linguist doesn't have to be fluent in other languages, or even write very well in his or her own language. Studying and doing are different. But historically and today, in the field of interpersonal communication, studying and doing are not totally separate.

In the West, the study of communication, under the name rhetoric, was part of the Trivium or "first three" of what came to be the seven classical liberal arts. And so from the beginning this field has been concerned with how to communicate, even though some of the most important figures in the field, such as Isocrates, were criticized as being more adept at telling others what to do than at doing it.[1] At any rate, for a long time there has been a tacit assumption that communication and the study of communication were part of the same thing. Most university courses today in "communication" or

[1] Which calls to mind Bernard Shaw's observation that "those who can, do; those who can't, teach;" (and those who can't teach, teach others how to teach!).

"speech communication" continue to combine these two concepts of the field. In this book we will be mainly concerned with the study of interpersonal communication rather than with "how to communicate." We cling to the hope that the two are not unrelated.

Norbert Wiener in *The Human Use of Human Beings* may have struck a nerve when he wrote of his dismay that "so many persons who have elected communication as a field of study have nothing to communicate." There is something wise and humane in the traditional communication or public speaking course in which students are obliged to express something worth saying as well as they can. Only in their decadent forms are such courses exercises in performance. The more recent trend to a broader view of communication to include much more than "stand-up public speaking" may have retained much of that spirit. Courses in "interpersonal communication" or "discussion" or "group dynamics" are sound only when what is communicated is substantial and meaningful to those who participate.

Some have said that the study of interpersonal communication should embrace at least four goals: the apprehension of sound theory and results of empirical research on communication; some awareness of methods for expanding on such research; greater sensitivity toward others with whom one communicates and sensitivity to the process of communication; and, if the word does not sound out of fashion, skills in the ability to participate in communication, whether speaking, listening, or facilitating discussions.

In short, courses in communication as represented in the tradition of "speech" or "speech-communication" departments have attempted to span both the analytical and the creative goals of education, and when one considers other academic disciplines, it is clear that such an attempt is remarkable. We could put this another way: historically and today, interpersonal communication studies embrace the traditions of the humanities and the contemporary concerns represented in the social sciences. The potential strength drawn from two traditions, however, runs the constant risk of becoming the weakness of a division between the two, for if the two are not mutually exclusive they at least give emphasis to different standards that are not always compatible.

We might briefly note some of the distinctions, which in combination might strengthen our understanding of communication but which in opposition may fragment it. One consideration is the choice of what to consider worth studying in the first place. The humanistic tradition has tended to focus on major events—speeches, or social movements. The social science tradition not only has favored smaller units, but has actively created its own subjects of study, as in experimental studies. It might also be said that the humanities tradition has stressed the great achievements of human beings—the great art, great speeches, great dramas; the social sciences to a surprising extent have focused more on the failures, the problems, the deviant or socially disapproved activities. Similarly, both the subject matter and the results of studies in the humanities tend to be unique; one rhetorical analysis does not make another obsolete; one is free to "do an Aristotelian analysis" of events today if one chooses to. In the social sciences, modeled on the natural sciences, things are different; we find no Aristotelian studies of, say, group leadership in an urban gang. Another apparent difference is in the area of "choice": humanistic studies of communication, past and present, have given a place for individual choice in what is said or done. The social sciences tradition, while not denying individual choice, has tended to stress pressures, forces, or at least probabilities of what will happen. If we were to go further with such comparisons we could mention the use of emotive language or statistics in the writing of studies.

I suppose it might be said that a model student of interpersonal communication could appreciate both traditions and see them as complements rather than as opponents. One might even hope for the day when, as was true not so very long ago, there will not be such pronounced divisions, when there will be no distinction between science and philosophy. But at present we must recognize these two traditions when trying to begin a study of interpersonal communication.

An earlier draft of this book was submitted to several scholars for their comments and suggestions. One scholar said, in effect, "The book will be all right if you remove all of the social science stuff and concentrate on interpersonal communication from the dramatic perspective." Another reviewer, coming from a different tradition, urged that much more attention be given to empirical studies and the methodologies currently employed so that students would appreciate the study of communication as a science. My concern is not so much with the final shape of this book, which may disappoint scholars of both persuasions, as with the study of interpersonal communication, which might finally be directed one way or the other for purposes of purity or modernity or consistency. Now more than ever before we need to view our communicating from many perspectives. Individually, each of us may favor one or another vantage point, but we may be missing something if we are blind to or fail to communicate with one who sees things from another point of view. The study of human communication may be the oldest academic study. If we are open to the multiple perspectives of the study today, we may also be participating in the most modern of studies.

Special thanks go to the anonymous scholars who read and commented on an earlier draft of this book and to Lloyd C. Chilton at Macmillan for his encouragement and assistance throughout the preparation of the book. The selection from *Love Story* by Erich Segal is included with the kind permission of Harper and Row, Publishers, Inc.

J. C. C.

CONTENTS

THREE

For Example . . . 61

FOUR

We Speak the Same Language 71

FIVE

Not in So Many Words 97

Contents

ONE

MORE THAN
MEETS THE EYE

Look at the sketch above. What do you see? Be cautious. If you are very careful you might say something like: "lines printed on a page." If that seems too cautious, then perhaps: "a drawing of two people." But if that seems uninformative then there are other interpretations: "two college students having coffee." Or, "Some couple—I think they're living together, but I'm not sure. It looks like they've been studying or are going to study. He seems mad at her, but maybe he's thinking about his exams. . . ." And there are many more possibilities, of course, limited mostly by our own imagination. But how free are we to imagine whatever we want to imagine? Where do we draw the line between being sufficiently objective and overly subjective?

If we are looking at a drawing and answer "lines on a page" or listen to a conversation and identify only sounds and pauses, we may be too cautious to understand very much about an iffy subject like interpersonal communication. On the other hand, if we give answers like "she's mad at him but he's just thinking of his exam," probably we are not cautious enough. We are inferring a great deal from a limited amount of information and we may be saying more about our own experiences or our own suspicions than about what we can possibly know. You might say that the first sort of cautious guess is very objective, maybe too objective; the last kind of guess, which will differ somewhat for each interpreter, we might say is too subjective.

Even that middle view, "a drawing that shows two figures," involves some degree of subjectivity; there are no "people" on the page. We *sense* the lines through our sensory apparatus (in this case our eyes only, though in most real life situations we utilize many senses at once). But to make the image meaningful, we must go far beyond that sense data. We, the perceivers, must *make* sense of what we see.

The "sensing" of a drawing is rather simple compared to interpersonal communication. How is it that we sense a tone of hostility or friendliness in a voice, or a double meaning of an apparently simple statement, or sense what a person is driving at in a round-about conversation, or sense that this person is telling the truth and that person is lying, or sense that it is time to leave a party, or sense that Martha likes Ted more than Ted likes Martha? Certainly we don't come to the conclusions by "sense data" or physical stimuli alone.

Sensing the stuff of interpersonal communication, making sense of that, and being sensible about it: that is what we would like to be able to do. Certainly this book cannot tell anybody exactly what to observe and how to make sense of any situation. But we can try to give some guidance to try to be more sensible about what we seem to do so naturally. We will begin with the ways in which we seem to make sense of what we perceive around us, for to a considerable extent the study of interpersonal communication is a complex exercise in perception. Whether you are mostly interested in your day to day conversations or hope to conduct research on the communication behavior of others, these simple matters of perception are equally important. We will begin with what is perhaps the simplest, most familiar concept.

Figure and Ground

Any elementary book on perception will probably mention the words *figure* and *ground* (or *background*). The figure is what a person focuses on, what stands out for that person. What it stands out against is the ground. Probably the most famous illustration of this is the half-century-old "faces and vase" drawing.

In this simple form, you may focus your attention on the white part of the drawing, in which case you can see the figure as a vase or goblet, but if you focus your attention on the black part of the drawing, you are likely to perceive the silhouettes of two people. In this case the black faces are the figure, the white center is the ground. At least as interesting as the illusion of seeing first a vase and then faces is the extreme difficulty of seeing both at the same time. Lesson: to perceive anything requires both background and figure. This is all very elementary, all very familiar to you. The more technical explanation of why this is so—psychologically and physiologically—is not so simple. [1]

There are other perceptual phenomena, apart from such contrived optical illusions, with which we may all be familiar. One of the best examples is in photography. Usually the simplest, cheapest, and most foolproof cameras are those which contain small, fixed lenses that cannot be adjusted. Point the camera in the right direction, click the shutter, and assuming there is sufficient light, the developed picture will be clear with everything in focus. But that is precisely the disadvantage of such cameras; the photographer cannot focus an image so that what he or she feels is the most important subject is sharply defined against a background that is blurred. Rather, everything with such a camera—the face of your friend, the trees, the clouds—will be equally in focus. Our eyes and other sensing organs, in contrast, are more like the cameras with adjustable lenses. We must choose what to focus on and what to "blur" into foreground or background. A good photographer is not merely an experienced technician using superior equipment; the good photographer, like any artist or sensitive observer, shares with others by making choices that his film records. Thus it is a mistaken notion that "pictures tell the truth" or merely record "what is there"; photographs no less than any other record of perception reveal choices of emphasis and choices of background.

We might also note, in passing, the perceived records of events as conveyed by a newspaper or television or radio news program. The news media is sometimes criticized for giving too much attention to some items ("news means bad news") while ignoring or "blurring" other stories. But the opposite criticism should also be noted. If, in the fixed time slot for a news presentation, every story of riots, weather, elections, and sports scores receives equal attention, the result may be even worse.

In principle, how we focus our attention in a study of interpersonal communication is not very different. If we listen to every sound of

[1] For a slightly technical but very readable introduction to the biological and physiological aspects of perception, see Otto Lowenstein, *The Senses*, (Middlesex, England and Baltimore: Penguin Books, Ltd., 1966). Also highly recommended is Bernard Berelson and Gary Steiner, *Human Behavior: An Inventory of Findings* (New York: Harcourt Brace Jovanovich, 1964), Chapter 4, "Perceiving."

every word, the larger patterns and context of a conversation may be a blur. If we try to sense the mood or the overall tone, we will probably have to ignore every little sound.

When we are with a good friend, what will we pay most attention to or focus on—*each word?* Probably not. If we have trouble hearing, as on a bad connection on a long distance call, we might give more attention to each word. Or if the person speaks with a certain dialect or with an accent that makes his words difficult for us to understand, we might give extra attention to each successive word, but not usually. We listen to *phrases* and *whole sentences*—if our friend actually talks in whole sentences. More likely than not, we can guess ahead of time, sometimes, how the sentence will end and maybe even what the next sentence will be. Sometimes *tone of voice* is more important than the words and sentences themselves. Whatever the literal content of the sentences, the tone may mean that he or she is happy or miffed or troubled. There is much more to consider: facial expressions, gestures, the time and place where we are talking, the movement of the eyes, the physical movement of our friend, closer or further from us, or turning and walking away, and on and on.

All of the possibilities that we will be considering throughout this book may be at some time the figure or focal point for us, or may only be the background. It depends on the situation. Even in attempting to conduct empirical studies of interpersonal communication, the researcher must decide how to sort out what he wishes to focus on against some background in order to perceive clearly what had gone unnoticed before. But once more the lesson: when communicating with others or when studying how others seem to be interacting we cannot focus on everything, we cannot eliminate all background by bringing everything to the fore.

More importantly, different people are likely to treat different aspects of the communication as figure and ground, and it is not always easy to recognize who is concentrating on what. Three guys at college like the same music, dress in similar clothes, wear their hair at about the same length, and "rap." The music, the clothes, and the hair are all background for them, perhaps, against which the rapping is the figure. One goes home and finds "he just can't communicate" with his parents; his parents show with their eyes and maybe with their words that they are focusing on that music, those clothes, that hair.

People who really get along are often people who, quite literally, "see things the same way."

Selective Perception

"Seeing is also a way of not seeing," Kenneth Burke observed. Seeing the figure means not seeing the background. But obviously what we "see" is not simply a matter of adjusting the lenses of our eyes or pricking up our ears. We are quite selective in what we see or hear. Much of this is more psychological than physical. Two people with measurably identical abilities to see and hear do not necessarily see and hear the same thing. If their interests and past experiences are different, if one is hungry and one just ate, if one is exhausted and the other hyped up with coffee, if one is in a good mood and the other in a bad mood, they are likely to perceive the same thing—whatever it might be—in somewhat different ways.

The concept known as *selective perception* is a basic concept in the theory of perception, in a study of interpersonal communication, and certainly in our own habits of communication as well. We will be returning to this idea many times throughout the book, but before going on, try a simple exercise using the same drawing we saw before on page 1.

Imagine for a few minutes that you are the layout editor for a publishing company and that you are obliged to use this drawing or parts of it for different publications with different purposes. Take four strips of paper or envelopes or cards that can be used as a frame to block off certain parts of the drawing. Let us say that you want to use part of the drawing to illustrate these stories:

1. Youth: The Hope of Tomorrow.
2. Mental Illness Strikes One in Ten.
3. Love Is a Four Letter Word.
4. Boredom.
5. I Was an Informer for the C.I.A.

This sort of exercise (cropping) is sometimes performed in preparing a photograph for publication. Film makers and television directors

do the same sort of thing in selecting the appropriate distance and angle to achieve the desired effect. And, analogously, we perform the same sort of exercise, unthinkingly, nearly every moment of the day. We, no less than the editor or director, are performing a creative act; we are not merely taking in or presenting "what is there." We select, we disregard, we focus, and in sharing such choices for perception with others we offer a point of view, a tacit judgment of what is to be regarded as important and not important.

Later in the book we will consider some of the dominant models or metaphors that have been used to help organize our concepts of interpersonal communication. Two of these models, that of the drama and that of games, should be discussed briefly in connection with the above exercise.

How, for example, does one regard a feeling like boredom? One might be bored when one is alone, or one might be bored when with somebody else. One might want to give an impression of being bored for some ulterior purpose—to indicate to another than he or she should stop talking, for example, or to convey an impression of a difference between the two ("You might find that interesting, but I find it boring . . ."). Viewed in such ways, boredom is an act or a ploy, a small piece of a larger sequence of events between persons, who can be regarded as participating in a human drama or a game. How to express boredom then becomes more complex. We have choices—with posture, hands, eyes, facial expressions, and so on.

Thus we have choices in how we use that drawing, just as in life we have and display choices in expressing a feeling like boredom. We might go further. Shall we try to evoke in the viewer of the drawing a similar feeling, a feeling of boredom? Shall we try to bore the viewer or try to make the viewer really interested in boredom? In considering such alternatives we quickly realize that any choice of what to express is bound up in other choices and assumptions of human interaction. We make our choices largely on the assumption that others share the same tacit understandings, for there is no meaning in any expression of the face, the hands, the voice, the words, apart from our shared assumptive meanings in any given context. The focusing, the blurring, the cropping, and the captions contribute to that context.

One question raised in this exercise is that of the effect of a particular label on our perception? If, instead of acting as an editor, we were a *reader*, and if we saw the caption "Boredom," along with a portion of the drawing, how would that label influence our perception?

If you are introduced to a person and told he "has an IQ of 180," or "is a high school drop-out," or "just returned from China," or "is 'gay,' " what influence does such a label have on your perception of the stranger? From both experience and many studies, we know that such labels greatly influence our perceptions, our attitudes, and our subsequent behavior.[2] As we will discuss shortly, in many ways we introduce our own labels in the process of communication, not only directly through what we may say, but more subtly through the clothes we wear, the posture we adopt, our style of speaking, and so on. We are selective in what we perceive *and* to a considerable extent on the ways we try to influence the selective perceptions of others.

Filling In and Getting Organized

There are a few other basic principles in perception that we ought to get used to. One concept that goes by various names refers to our need

---

[2] See John Condon, *Semantics and Communication*, 2nd ed. (New York: Macmillan, 1975), especially Chapters 2–4.

to organize our perceptions into recognizable forms. At the beginning of the chapter, it was this in part that converted "lines on a page" into "two people," and "a table," and so on. As with other aspects of perception, our ability to organize is partly the result of our human perceptual apparatus, and thus "universal," and partly the result of our experience and learning. Anthropologists have occasionally reported incidents in which a person who had never before seen a photograph was unable to recognize the glossy patterns of lighter and darker shades as representing anything. Persons who have been unable to see from birth but who are able to see after undergoing an operation (for cataracts, for example) are sometimes totally bewildered by what is suddenly visible.[3] Often, apparently, it takes much time and painful learning to be able to make sense of the visual world they had imagined before the operation. More familiar to all of us is our learning the language of the mass media—radio, film, television. We can usually distinguish immediately a program from a commercial. We learn the possible meanings of a dissolve, or juxtaposition; we learn to recognize a flashback or the indicators of the passing of time. We have learned this, but not everybody has. In my own experience I have seen East African farmers watching a film that they could recognize as a representation of people doing things, but lacking sophistication in film techniques they were baffled by the man on the screen seemingly changing his costume in just a fraction of a second.

Or consider the now familiar examples first presented by the Gestalt perception psychologists many years ago. They found that we are more likely to perceive this: ⋰ as a triangle than as three separate dots, or this figure: ∷ as a square rather than four dots. The need to combine, to organize, in perception is strong: perception is the economy of thought. Also, we do not seem to like forms that appear incomplete. Many people get edgy looking at something like this:

this is it

Write that on a blackboard and see how long it takes before somebody corrects it.

---

[3] Colin Cherry, *On Human Communication* (New York: Science Editions, John Wiley and Sons, 1961), p. 261.

Try to recall any film or television program you have recently seen. Think of one small sequence of about a minute's duration. It is not so difficult to recall the meaning or the impression of that scene. But to remember exactly *what* you were *shown visually* is quite difficult, for most of what we remember is what *we* have filled in, not what was presented to us. Little wonder the eyewitness reports of persons who were at the scene of an accident are so often distorted. This is not to condemn memory or inattention to detail, for life might be impossible if we perceived and recalled only the sense data presented to us, without organizing it into meaningful patterns. To organize, to make meaningful, to make sense of what otherwise would seem fragmentary is normal behavior.

But what of the person who "sees" that strangers are always looking at him, who "sees" that people seem to follow him, that waiters are nasty, that bus drivers don't stop for him sometimes, that children seem to run away when he approaches? He, too, has formed patterns that are meaningful to him, that make sense to him. A psychiatrist forms these "symptoms" into yet another pattern that makes sense to the psychiatrist. We label the psychiatrist "normal"; we label his poor patient "mentally ill." And our labeling we label as "normal behavior." [4]

Psychological Set and the Definition of the Situation

Yet another useful working concept here is that of *set* or *expectancy set*. This is the "set" of "being all set" to do something, the "set" in "get ready, get set," so that you can go without further thought. As in the other explanations of basic terms, there is a certain awkwardness about emphasizing something so familiar with a label. If you understand the idea or "set," then you realize that you always have some "set" or another about any situation. To prepare your set to understand set, we will use a dramatic example. Just suppose that you are living in a room by yourself, and that every day when you leave your room you are careful to close and lock the door. Now suppose that

[4] See, for example, Thomas Szasz, *The Myth of Mental Illness: Foundations of a Theory of Personal Conduct* (New York: Hoeber-Harper, 1961).

one day you return to your room—all set to relax after a hard day's work. Usually, you would enter the room, flip on the light, and do whatever you planned to do in your familiar surroundings. You would perceive only a fraction of what you might have perceived the first time you rented the room, for you know what is there. Your actions would be mostly habitual, predictable.

But just suppose that on this day you return to your room and find the door slightly ajar and a light on in the room. And just assume that you are *sure* that you closed the door and turned off the light as you always do. And further assume that the landlady would never, in your speedy analysis of the situation, have entered or left the door open and the light on. In short, suppose you face what should have been familiar and comforting, but now seems to be somehow wrong and anything but comforting. Your "set" is probably going to be quite different this time. You may enter with unusual caution, you may call out to see if somebody is in your room. There is no answer. Now you listen carefully to see if you can hear any movement within. Nothing. Quickly, you look first for your valuables—a radio or stereo or typewriter. You notice things: a drawer partly open, objects where you did not remember leaving them. Assume, now, in this hypothetical example, that you *had* left a light on and did *not* close the door all the way, and that therefore *nothing* was changed or rearranged in your room and that *no* intruder had entered. You will still be responding to a very different perception of the room because of your changed "set" toward that room.

We have somewhat different expectancy sets for almost any situation—a party, the first day of class, an exam, a date, opening a long-awaited letter or what looks like an advertisement. We have odd sets, some of us, while riding in an elevator with only one other person or flying in a plane. Our mood, our experience, our expectations will influence what we perceive, how we act or react. Everything we perceive is perceived through some set, and any set is partly influenced by what we perceive.

The labels applied to situations—described by others or self-labeled—reflect and often influence our set toward the situation. "This is going to be fun," or "this is really important." There are some comedians whose very appearance evokes a set to laugh. But if some jerk at a party says, "I heard a really funny joke—you'll die laughing at this . . ." we may adopt a set that seems to say, "Oh, sure, let's see if you can make me laugh." Much "prejudice" is an expression of negative or defensive sets toward certain people.

Physical settings, the design of a building or a room, are attempts to provide a particular "set": banks that look like Greek temples exude a cold feeling of permanence and austerity so that some persons prefer to go to the friendly Neighborhood Savings and Loan; standardized fast food restaurants that attempt to build in a set of fun or simply efficiency and cleanliness. Incense or airwick, candles or strobe lights, rock music or chamber music contribute to different sets for people who enter a particular setting.

Once again the terminology of the drama is useful. The set in the theatre is an artificial construction appropriate to the setting in which the drama occurs. This in turn provides a psychological set for the viewers. But more than this, set and setting provide a part of the context within which the actions will be played out and give specific meaning to those actions. The meaning of a young girl's smile when she stands before a Christmas tree is not the same as when she stands in the corner of her schoolroom. The setting is not a mere backdrop against which actions are played, but rather it contributes to the meanings of those actions.

We may assume that in the routine of daily life there is an appropriateness or congruity between what happens and where it takes place. When the two are incongruous, we find or create new meanings, as in surrealistic paintings of familiar objects amidst a desert landscape. At a recent international conference on hunger in the world, the wire services carried a story of the Bangladesh delegate's appeal being drowned out by the noise of a cocktail party given by another delegation in the adjacent room. We might assume that it was the perceived incongruity itself that seemed to amplify the sounds of clinking glasses from the next room. In any case, these sounds and what they appeared to symbolize were not merely background or noise; they altered the significance of the words spoken by the representative of Bangladesh and, ironically, may have turned a routine conference report into an international news story.

In recent years, as the language of the advertiser and public relations people has entered the public vocabulary, there has been considerable talk about "images." People discuss the image of a political candidate—Johnson had his folksy image and his wheeler-dealer image; Nixon had a loser image and then talked publicly about changing his image into the new Nixon.[5] Particularly when there is very little difference between political candidates or products, it seems there is some need to create an illusion of something special and attractive, or if nothing else, to try to alter or soften bad images. This term *image* is very closely related to the concept of set. If, for example, an airline can create a particular image of "safety first" or "friendliness" or "sexy stewardesses," it provides a particular set for the passengers. Advertising appeals, personnel uniforms, and other public expressions will help sustain that image. The hope is that the passenger who expects "safety first" or "friendly skies" or even "sexy stewardesses" will tend to perceive what he expects. What you see is what you get, but also what you see depends on what you are set to see.

Understandably, the public has grown somewhat distrustful if not cynical about some image-building attempts that are very transparent. But not everybody who might be critical of political candidates or oil companies is quite as critical of their own simpler attempts to create a certain image, to provide a certain set for others, toward their own activities or toward themselves.

Clothing often contributes to a set. The robes of a judge or the uniform of a cop are intended to evoke some mood of authority for those who encounter them. In the celebrated case of the Chicago Seven, arising out of disturbances at the Democratic Party's National Convention in 1968, the one act of contempt of court that disturbed even a more lenient appeals judge was the appearance of Jerry Rubin and Abbie Hoffman in court in mock judicial robes. And if one's uniform or other clothing contributes to the set of others and, collectively to the setting itself, the clothes are also likely to influence, as we shall consider later, the set of those who wear them.

These simple concepts of perception—figure and ground, selective perception, organizing the disparate into some concrete impression that is meaningful, and set—can be combined into a single more gen-

---

[5] Joe McGinniss, *The Selling of the President, 1968* (New York: The Trident Press, 1969).

eral but useful concept: the definition of the situation. When we attempt to define a word, we express something of its significance in other words. If our definition is well chosen, we ignore many other possible definitions that would apply only in other usages. The idea of a "definition of a situation" is not very different. When we define a situation, we express something of its significance not in words but in many aspects of our inner attitudes and outward behavior.

Try, if you will, to define the situation where you are now. Or recall any class that you are attending. Recall, if you can, the arrangement of the desks, the placement and size of the chalkboard, the person who stands in front while everybody else sits. Maybe there is a bell or buzzer that punctuates the beginning and end of the class period. Think about the sounds of conversation before and after class and compare them with the style and tone of voice of that person in front of the rest of you, the scratches on the desk, the smell of the room, the aura of energy—such as it is. Such impressions are a part of a general definition of a classroom. They may have little to do with definitions that might be found in a dictionary or in a college catalogue or in some book on the philosophy of education. But they are likely to have a great deal to do with your set, what you notice and ignore, and much more that is a part of communication in that situation. This is not to say that any such definition is only the background for what transpires. It is part of the communication, it influences as well as reflects what happens and what does not. Only when we attempt to isolate some aspects—a conversation in the back row, or that person who almost always seems to arrive late, or the one who sits up front and always asks questions and gives opinions—do we regard that broadly defined situation as background. Figure and ground are rarely stable and fixed. Our focus shifts, and the study of communication is a study of shifting focuses.

But we can also assume that there are patterns even in these shifts of focus. Communication may be a process, but it cannot be totally random and still be communication. A process, yes, but one on which we—as participants in communication and as students of communication—will impose some kind of structure and find (or impose) segmentations.

Segmentation

Ray L. Birdwhistell, whose pioneering work in nonverbal communication has helped to alter the whole notion of communication, has written: "an individual does not communicate; he engages in or becomes part of communication. . . . In other words, he does not originate communication; he participates in it." [6] You read this sentence and in a popular sense the words seem to "communicate to you." But where does the communication begin? It is certainly not merely by my writing the words—but also in the background and motivation that led me to write them. More than that, however, they have some meaning for you and for me because they are written in a language that we share. And in that sense we are "participating in" communication in English. We did not originate that language; nobody did. It evolved into its present state and continued to change, and even its beginning can be marked only arbitrarily.

We see a girl smiling. We could say that she communicates a smile, but in another sense she did not originate that smile at that moment—the smile like the spoken language also arose in her background, her perception of the situation, the social and cultural expectations placed upon her in this situation, and so on. Without getting quite so philosophical we could say that her smile originated at least as much in another's previous remark or other behavior as in her own response.

Nearly everybody at one time or another has experienced thinking about somebody, then heard the telephone ring, picked up the phone, and—sure enough—the caller is the person you were thinking of. Amazing! *I was just thinking of you!* Parapsychologists, the people who study extrasensory perception and kindred phenomena, might say that in some of these cases the telepathy system just worked more speedily than the telephone system. Perhaps. Another explanation, for some of these incidents, is that the same constellation of events that led you to expect a call also worked to prompt your friend to call. In any case, when did the communication begin? When you started

---

[6] Ray L. Birdwhistell, "Contribution of Linguistic-Kinesic Studies to the Understanding of Schizophrenia," in *Schizophrenia, An Integrated Approach*, ed. Alfred Auerback (New York: The Ronald Press, Co., 1959), p. 104.

thinking of your friend? When the phone rang and, with that expectancy set, you answered the phone? Or when you picked up the phone and said "hello?" Or when your friend answered your "hello" and made it clear that your hunch was correct?

Keep in mind that we are asking these questions in order to decide when we should say that communication began *for the purpose of studying communication.* Our answer, whatever it is, will be an arbitrary choice, an imposed point of beginning, *not* an answer about when communication *really* began. In this case it may be most practical to mark the beginning as the point at which "you" picked up the telephone, for at that point your behavior and that of any background sounds that added to a definition of your situation were perceivable by the other party.

There are some weaknesses in this approach. If your friend phoned and there was no answer, he could conclude that you were not home, or were not in the mood to answer the phone, or were in the bathroom, and so some might want to say that even the "no answer" is a kind of behavior that communicates. This is a valid observation.

When does interpersonal communication end? Take the last example and imagine having talked on the phone for a few minutes, and then hanging up. If you continue to think about things said and things left unsaid in the telephone conversation, are you still "communicating"? In this book, for purposes of studying interpersonal communication, we would like to say no, mainly because it is very difficult to study the sort of mental behavior that is not directly perceivable by the person with whom you would be communicating. But if this seems satisfactory for the case of hanging up a telephone, what about a conversation in a hallway that ends with the two people walking away from each other? One turns and looks back at the other. Has communication ended? Here I would want to say no, at least not if the person can view the other's walking behavior and interpret something from it—that the person is angry, sad, or hurrying. Interpretations made on the basis of that sort of behavior can be more easily observed and studied. Indeed, people do sometimes stomp off after a conversation with the hope that others will see that behavior and "get the message."

The points we choose as the beginning and end of individual segments or acts of communication are arbitrary. The concept of a *per-*

ceptual field has been used by social psychologists for some time as a basis for including or excluding observable phenomena. A person who would study small group interaction—and there are thousands of such studies—must decide at some point what is "a group" and what is not. Are all of the people on a public beach "a group" or just a crowd that includes many small groups? Most would say the latter because a person on the beach is only aware of some of the other people around him or her, not all of them. Those people who are within the individual's perceptual field may be identified as part of a single group. That is the sort of distinction we are proposing here.

As we attempt to impose our own markers to segment aspects of the continual flow of behavior, we must keep in mind that the people involved are themselves likely to segment that behavior differently, so again we must not confuse the study of interpersonal communication with communication itself. Like a visitor in a new land to whom "all these natives look alike," when we are outside of the communication situation we may find it very difficult to perceive it as one within would. Maybe it really takes one to know one.

Patterns

Learning to speak a language means, in part, learning to imitate sounds. At one time it was thought that language development was primarily the result of imitation of what we heard. Now it is realized that although imitation is important, what we especially do is learn to imitate *patterns*—so that each of us says things that have never been said before in quite that way.[7] From the basic patterns we generate new utterances. Learning about some subject, whether it is astronomy or interpersonal communication, also means, for the most part, discovering patterns. A good theory is one that describes a pattern so well that it serves to predict what will occur, assuming that patterns are consistent and do not change for our having discovered them. Many academic tests that are used to determine which students are brighter or better able to learn than others are pattern tests. There is an as-

[7] Eric Lenneberg, *The Biological Foundations of Language* (New York: John Wiley and Sons, 1967).

sumption that those who can catch on to underlying patterns are more adept than those who cannot. This book, too, is largely about patterns—patterns of interpersonal communication. Our goal, however, is not so much to describe certain patterns as to attempt to offer pointers for finding such patterns in communication.

Perceiving patterns is not a simple matter of education or even intelligence. Much depends upon matters we have already mentioned—what one focuses on, what one expects to perceive. Consider the following problem in pattern perception, which should not be too difficult, as it is used as an entrance examination for kindergarten children.[8] It is not very easy, however, for many apparently intelligent and well-educated adults.

The Problem: Based on the pattern shown here, determine which of the remaining letters of the alphabet should be placed above the line and which should be placed below the line:

A   EF   HI KL

    BCD   G   J

If you cannot find the pattern, turn to the foot of this page for the explanation. Then compare your set toward the problem with that of the Japanese kindergarten children who were able to solve it.

Patterns in communication take many forms. One is the content, the need to determine which of two or more patterns seems more reasonable. Judges and juries often listen to evidence presented by two different lawyers, one for the prosecution, one for the defense. Rarely are the two versions *totally* different. What does differ significantly is the interpretation of the evidence, the order of presentation, and the emphasis. One leads to the inescapable conclusion that the accused is guilty, the other leads to a reasonable doubt that the accused is guilty.

---

[8] For the past thirty years, the Japanese education system has become extraordinarily competitive, the emphasis being on getting into the best schools. These pressures on the student begin even before kindergarten with interviews and a battery of tests such as this one.

The letters written above the line are all made with straight lines; those below all contain some curved lines.

It is up to the judge or the jury members to determine which pattern makes more sense.

In a classical model for argumentation, dating before the time of Aristotle, a student of communication was asked to consider the fight between a giant and a dwarf. How would a lawyer defend each man if a judge asked who started the fight? In defense of the dwarf the lawyer might argue: "Would this *little* man ever be so foolish as to fight with such a huge man as this giant? Of course not. Obviously the giant must have started the fight." Conversely, the lawyer could defend the giant by saying, "Would this giant of a man ever stoop so low as to fight with this little man? Of course not. Obviously the dwarf started the fight." Which pattern of reasoning is more reasonable?

A class complains that they are doing poorly because they have no motivation to study: the teacher's lectures are dull, the material is boring, and the teacher doesn't seem to care whether the class learns anything or not. But their teacher complains, "My students are dull, they never study the material, so they make it impossible for me to teach them well." Again, there are two interpretations, two patterns.

In the case of lawyers arguing a case, we might assume that each will try to present a pattern that most favors his client. The good lawyer seeks to create or impose a pattern upon the evidence in order to be persuasive. But what of the two versions of the "dull class"—the students' version and the teacher's version? Perhaps this case is not so different. Each side attempts to see things in the way that is most self-serving. Still, an outsider who wished to be neutral or objective would have to recognize that both interpretations are plausible and, indeed, both may be correct. Certainly in this case both could work together to create the unhappy situation.

Are such patterns discovered or are they imposed? It is not always easy to say. In many cases this is a moot question. Anthropologists ask the same sort of question when attempting to describe a culture: is the culture *in the people* observed, or is the culture in the *anthropologist* who wants to organize what he observes? Linguists ask similar questions about languages studied—are the rules in the language, or are the rules in the linguist who seeks to describe them? And we must consider the same question in trying to describe what happens when people engage in activities lumped under the heading "interpersonal communication." We should be aware of what seems to be a human need to find patterns.

In an ingenious experiment conducted by Professor Alex Bavelas [9] at Stanford University, volunteers were instructed in the use of a device consisting of several push buttons. They were asked to try to discover the appropriate sequence of buttons that, if pushed in the right order, would activate a buzzer. In fact, the buttons were not connected to anything and there was no proper sequence. However, the experimenter would, during the course of the volunteer's efforts, buzz the buzzer with increasing frequency in order to create the illusion that the volunteer had actually discovered some predetermined pattern. The remarkable effect of this experiment was not simply that the volunteers thought that they had indeed discovered a pattern, but that nearly all remained convinced that they had even after the deception was explained to them. No explanation would convince them until they assisted the experimenter and observed similar reactions in other volunteers. Some scholars have found the implications of this simple experiment profoundly disturbing because so much of scholarship is the search for patterns.

Yet one man's "discovery" is another man's "projection." This seems especially true of a conversation in which one listener may seem to catch on to what a person is trying to say better than another listener—or sometimes even better than the speaker himself. To a considerable extent the role of a counselor or therapist, or even a good friend or relative, is that of a perceiver of patterns that the troubled person may not even be aware of. However, the risk of amateur psychology is to impose or project too much, a risk we should be especially careful of in a study of interpersonal communication.

It is extremely important to recognize the need and ability to find or create patterns. Without patterns there would be no meaning, no communication. And yet if we accept every pattern that occurs to us, every pattern we impose or project onto others without regard to realities, we are only talking to ourselves and are maybe a little bit mad.

[9] John C. Wright, *Problem Solving and Search Behavior Under Non-Contingent Rewards.* Unpublished doctoral thesis, Stanford University, 1960; cited in Paul Watzlawick, et al., *Pragmatics of Human Communication; A Study of Interactional Patterns, Pathologies, and Paradoxes* (New York: W. W. Norton, 1967), 263–264.

Levels of Communication

Our study of interpersonal communication will be aimed mostly at a common sense level. Common sense does not mean self-evident, though that may sometimes seem to be the case. Rather, we mean that we will be examining interpersonal communication primarily at the level of ordinary, or common, sense-data observation—mostly what we can see and hear. We will be mostly ignoring the psychological and the physiological processes we can only infer. We will also ignore for the most part the systems of language, of cultural values, of social structure, and the current tides of history that influence interpersonal communication. We are even going to ignore, except for some speculations near the end of the book, the possible *consequences* of some kinds of interpersonal communication, though according to some theorists that is where any such study should begin.

At times we run the risk of a serious mistake in attempting to describe or interpret a problem on one level that might be better described or interpreted on another level. Take the example of the break-up of a marriage. Two people we have known for a long time, who seemed so happy, announce that they have agreed to a divorce. It is fatuous to say that "they must have had trouble communicating," but certainly their patterns of communication might be studied to see where things went wrong and, possibly, if it is not too late, even to try to alter their behavior so that they remain married. This, after all, is what marriage counselors do. In other words, we could view each instance of a marriage break-up as a special case to be studied in and of itself. But because published statistics tell us that this is not an isolated case at all, perhaps this is not something to study on an individual level but at a regional or national level. We might look at changing values in the cultures, different attitudes about divorce, changing sexual standards, and the kinds of pressures that sometimes seem to make divorce more expected than an enduring marriage.

Any event that we might label interpersonal communication can be viewed on many levels, though even the separation into separate levels is somewhat artificial and arbitrary. One person could trace the history of two individuals who are participating in the communication and try to discern all of the events (or at least some of the major ones) that led up to the particular moment of the observed communication.

Another could describe the neurological responses of these individuals at that moment, or work with a psychologist in order to examine their psychobiological behaviors. A team of linguists could tell us something about why certain words were used and how the words conform to the rules of the language. They could, even more specifically, identify the maleness or femaleness of the speech and the dialect as being from a certain region, even within a certain period of time. Sociologists could explain why these two people were likely to encounter each other, and social psychologists might offer some insights into their likely social perceptions of each other. A cultural anthropologist might explain something of the cultural values that encouraged this particular interaction, and why it would be less likely or would have a different meaning in some other society. The contemporary historian or social critic might consider the encounter as but a piece of the current social fabric and note parallels with and some significant differences from other encounters at other times. Still others would want to add commentaries on the gestures, facial expressions, clothing, and what they signify; others might comment on the influence of technology on the interpersonal encounter.

Like the Buddhist belief that all of the world is contained in a grain of sand, the meaning that can be derived from the simplest human encounter radiates outward. There may be developed, some day, a grand theory that relates all of the levels so that we find constant principles of communication that help describe and explain everything from dream behavior to international peace negotiations. Some have sought something like this in what is known as "general systems theory." [10] But we will try to content ourselves with observing carefully more immediately perceivable behavior. That seems difficult enough.

Regardless of how we decide to segment units of communication or determine an appropriate level, there are some characteristics of interpersonal communication on which there is general agreement. [11]

[10] See, for example, Ludwig von Bertalanffy, *General Systems Theory* (New York: Brazi-ler, 1968).

[11] One of the clearest presentations of this is in Dean C. Barnlund, "Toward a Meaning Centered Theory of Communication," *Journal of Communication*, Vol. 12 (Dec. 1962), pp. 197–211.

One characteristic that seems self-evident—when pointed out—is that interpersonal communication as a process is irreversible. A child who taunts another is told, "You take that back!" But, of course, one cannot take back one's communication. One can apologize or say that he or she has had a change of mind, or say, "Of course I was just joking," or claim the other person misunderstood. But these remarks only continue the process. They do not erase or reverse it, and at times they make matters worse. Moreover, out of all of the interpersonal communicative behavior, only a small portion, if we were to quantify all such behavior, is likely to be meaningful to others with whom we are interacting. An individual has no final control over what others perceive, what interpretations they make, or within what frame of reference they make their interpretations. An individual may repeat certain words he thinks are important, emphasize them with a louder voice, with gestures, and so on, but he or she has no way of guaranteeing or even knowing that what was intended was what the other understood. In conversations with others, this recognition should make us more cautious in our expectations. In trying to describe and analyze the interpersonal communication of others, this should make us doubly cautious.

Conclusion

A word often used in discussing communication is the word *empathy*. To be empathetic or to have empathy toward another person is to be able to imagine how that person might be feeling or thinking, to attempt to see things from that person's point of view. (This is not quite the same as sympathy, because one can sympathize with somebody's plight without really understanding his situation very well.) Good listeners, we are sometimes told, empathize. Whatever else the elusive quality of empathy involves, at least it must include a large degree of projection. Although we sometimes say, "If I were you," what is more likely is something like: "If you were me in your situation." Most of what is meant by communication between people requires such an attitude. Empathy is a quality that cannot be taught, though presumably it must be learned. It is a personal quality that is expressed by many kinds of people, most of whom never heard of the field of interpersonal communication. But the analysis of communication, systems for classifying different communicative acts, techniques of identifying patterns of communicative behavior, and models and metaphors of communication that relate these terms and methods can be taught. The hope is that with a keener sense of awareness of the extraordinarily complex process of interpersonal communication, one can arrive at a better understanding and possibly a more empathetic sensitivity as well.

TWO
RELATIONSHIPS

Just the Two of Us Make Six

The late, charismatic Frederick "Fritz" Perls, who is credited with originating what is known as Gestalt therapy, wrote what has been called "The Gestalt Prayer:" [1]

> I do my thing, and you do your thing.
> I am not in this world to live up to your expectations
> And you are not in this world to live up to mine.
> You are you, and I am I,
> And if by chance, we find each other, it's beautiful.
> If not, it can't be helped.

As prayer or poetry or at least as expressing a theme in Gestalt therapy, Perls' words may be all right. But as a statement of the realities of interpersonal communication, it seems a bit too simple. Imagine for a moment that you are a male college student flying home for Christmas. Imagine that you have longish hair, a beard, and that you are

[1] Frederick S. Perls, *Gestalt Therapy Verbatim* (Moab, Utah: Real People Press, 1969), pp. 4.

wearing a ski jacket. If somebody asked you *who* you are, apart from your name, you might go into a long history of your background, interests, and maybe even your philosophy of life. Your beard and ski jacket might seem incidental or perhaps in some ways help you to express something of yourself. In any case, you have your own idea of who you are, and nobody else can ever quite know you as you know yourself.

But there you are boarding the plane. Suppose now that there are only a few remaining vacant seats and you have to quickly choose one. Which person do you choose to sit next to. You opt for a man about your father's age. Let us suppose that he is balding, sports no beard, and is dressed in a dark suit. That is your first impression of him, but if you think further you might be able to make some guesses about who he is and what your ensuing conversation or lack of it might be like.

That man, like you, has his own knowledge of himself, his own idea of who he is that he can never fully share with anybody else. His self-concept, like your image of yourself, may be idealized or overly modest—from the point of view of others. But whatever the image, it is largely personal and inaccessible to anybody else.

And just as you form an image of who he might be, he also forms some impressions of you as you sit down next to him. He might have a son your age and identify you with his own boy. He might not. He might think of you only as a person who took the seat he was hoping would remain vacant. Or he might be happy that you have come to help pass the time.

Thus far we have considered four kinds of images for the two people: each has an image of himself, and each has some sort of image or impression of the other. To these four we might add at least two more.

Along with your impression of the gentleman on the plane, you may have an impression of how he will think of you. You can't know, of course, but this might be a factor in deciding where to sit. So one more image is your idea of his idea of who you are. And a sixth image would be the converse, his idea of your idea of who he thinks he is.

If we were to diagram this with an X and a Y, with X being you and Y being the older man, we could write:

X*x*—your image of yourself
Y*y*—his image of himself

Xy—his image of you (X as seen by y)
Yx—your image of him (Y as seen by x)
Xyx—your image of his image of you
Yxy—his image of your image of him

Now comes a more complicated question. Who will talk to whom? Which two of those six images will interact?

One guess would be this: your idea of who you are will talk to

your idea of who that man is; and his idea of who he is will talk to his idea of who you are.

And perhaps, after talking for some time, you change your idea of who he is to one that is closer to his idea of who he is; and similarly, he may change his idea of who you are to an image that is somewhat closer to your idea of who you are. Perhaps the process of communication that leads from strangers through acquaintances to friends and then to *good* friends is a process of steadily reducing those "six people" into only two.

Or, perhaps not. What we are trying to describe is not simply the difference between strangers talking and friends talking. Who I am, or think I am, or would like to be, or want to be treated as . . . is not static, even in communication with one other person. There are times when a person wants to be treated as well-informed on a certain subject, and other times when a person wants to be regarded as naive; there are times when a person wants to be generous, and other times when maybe we all need to be a little selfish. Moods, experiences, attitudes, and relationships change, especially when one is in high school and college. The college student who returns home after even a few months away may have some trouble communicating with his family because he sees himself as having changed and wants to be treated somewhat differently by his parents. At least this is one possible source of a commonly observed awkwardness in reunions of various kinds.

Childhood, adolescence, the teens, and college age are segmented periods of life in which we assume a person undergoes many changes. A person continuously seeks to find himself or herself, and thus self-images are in a period of flux. Messrs. Freud, Piaget, Giselle, Erikson, and Spock have helped us to understand these years. We sometimes speak of the first four to six years as the formative years, in which the most fundamental aspects of personality and character seem to be established.

More recently, however, has come the growing recognition that one's formulation of a self-image and style of life does not end during childhood. As a result of changes in society itself and systematic studies of adult life, psychologists now speak of major identity crises occurring in many men and women around the age of thirty. And later, still, roughly between the mid-thirties and early forties, there is often a great effort to change. Forty-five is seen by many people as the last chance to be one's own person.

Thus it seems that throughout most of one's life, even one's *own* self-image or self-concept—who one thinks he is or would like to be or would like to be thought of—is not a simple matter. To say that "I am I" and "You are you" suggests that each of us know ourselves and, by implication, that communication is getting to know others and for others to know us as we know ourselves. But if *I* am still in a process of change, uncertainty, and *you* are, too, then how do we get to know each other? How shall we communicate?

We often have some very good clues to guide us in knowing who a person thinks he is, or how a person expects to be regarded in a particular situation. Prior information about a person serves to provide us with some set toward that person either as an individual or as a type. We may be told that a person is shy, or has been ill; that a man is an olympic athlete, or is a hustler and to be regarded with suspicion; or that a woman is the daughter of the president of the university, or works as a topless blackjack dealer in San Francisco. Such information does not tell us what such people might think of themselves or how they might want to be regarded when talking with us, but such labels and their resulting sets for us are likely to influence our perceptions of them. Often, of course, we have no prior information and even when we do, the information may be incorrect or misleading.

Similarly, people may introduce such labels in conversation, or may lead a conversation in a direction that allows another person to infer certain information. And the labeling is expressed not only in speech; often clothing—a tailored suit or jeans and sweatshirt—will give many clues about how some people might see themselves or wish to be treated at a particular time.

One of the clearest expressions of this is the uniform, such as that of a gas station attendant or a waiter, which expresses outwardly the person's professional activity. In personality and self-image, of course, there are all kinds of gas station attendants, waiters, and other professionals, but these personal qualities may be mostly irrelevant in professional encounters.

Facial expressions, posture, ways of walking—downcast or sprightly—and other bodily expressions also provide clues. As we shall see later, some of these may be unconscious or even easily misinterpreted; others may be part of a calculated performance to announce to others, "I'm friendly," or "Watch out, I'm in a bad mood!"

Through social structure and cultural values, each society provides some general guidelines of how certain people ought to be regarded in ordinary encounters. Some societies have more fixed rules than others. For example, many societies in the world today, and presumably most societies in the past, have encouraged young people to treat older people with deference. Many societies have similar tacit rules about conversations between men and women; many still discourage most kinds of communication between strangers of opposite sexes in public. Some societies, such as that of India, still retain vestiges of a caste system that guide communication among strangers—person X must never approach person Y, though person Y may approach person X. In the United States our sad racial history has not been so different. Black menial help would always address their white employers as "Ma'm" or "Sir," but were called by first names in return. The individualistic and democratic system of values in the United States has tended to blur overt expressions of how a person should be seen by others. In communication we are all supposed to be equal regardless of race, age, sex, religion, and so on. But there are unstated rules that can be recognized if we look closely.

In any case, many daily encounters that go by the name *interpersonal communication* are between people who do not know each other very well and who do not wish to know much about each other. This is particularly true in urban, industrialized settings, where there is rather high mobility—people moving in and out with great frequency. Thus we may be more conscious of those "six people in a dialogue" when communication becomes more personal or when conversations must continue for many minutes or hours.

The length of time one spends talking to another person upon an initial encounter also reflects and guides social structure and self-perceptions. The United States is popularly known throughout the world as a society where people like to get down to business right away. An Italian actress remarked, "Americans do everything too fast—even making love!" In other societies even the conversations leading to a simple transaction, such as buying something or asking a plumber to repair a broken pipe, may take a very long time by North American standards. One explanation is that before a person can accept another person—as a customer or client or, even more so, as a partner in some activity—he must discover what kind of person he or she is. That is, there is a *personal* element that may even outweigh the purely business or professional role in an encounter. The person wants to sort out the other's "three faces" before going further. North Americans are more likely to value the division between personality and aspects of competence, and thus communication can be more efficient and less probing. At any rate, the length of time of a conversation is an indication of many things, including pace of life, personal involvement, and also the concern with the person as a person. Sometime, try to carefully record the length of time of separate acts of communication with each person you encounter during the day; you may be surprised by the brevity of most.

I Know That You Know That I Know That . . .

We can think of these "six people in a dialogue" in rather general terms of images, impressions, and personal sets, which any two people may have toward each other and toward themselves. Let us try to be more specific in order to present a more complex model based on this general principle.

Instead of thinking of images or impressions, let's think for a moment about the kind of information that can be observed directly or, under certain conditions, elicited through interviews or even questionnaires. Assume we have just met. And assume that you are wearing glasses. You know that you wear glasses. And I also know that you wear glasses. Some people are bothered about having to wear glasses, so *maybe* this has some influence on our conversation. Now suppose that I wear contact lenses. I know that I wear contact lenses, of course, but I cannot be sure whether you have noticed that I wear them. If you ask me, I will tell you that I do wear contact lenses. This is the sort of information that may or may not be observed or inferred but is not necessarily intended to be kept a secret—except, perhaps, by some movie stars or possibly by would-be student pilots. There is much more information that cannot be observed or inferred so easily, for example, birthdates. For many people most of the time this is not a secret, but for some people, it is a secret and the subject of a certain amount of deception, as when minors try to buy a drink at a bar, or when an older person applies for a job, or maybe when some people who want to get married feel they are too old or too young. There is still other information that people may know but may take great pains to keep secret: sex lives, drinking habits, criminal records, tax information, and so on. Most people probably have at least some such information they would prefer to keep secret.

There are two other kinds of information that are relevant here. One is information that other people know about a person that the person himself may not know. Some of this is the sort that "your best friend won't tell you," the scare information that certain advertisers play upon—body odors, disgusting personal habits, even mistakes in language usage. Or it could be more innocuous information—you see that the other person has a piece of spinach on her teeth or that a man's fly is open—that the person may not become aware of until some time later. (There are many jokes of embarrassment that make much of this sort of thing.) There is also specialized information that only one's dentist or doctor or parents, perhaps, know. And finally there is information that even you don't know about you—and nobody else does either. Theoretically, I suppose, this is the largest of the categories, and for our purposes the least important.

Two psychologists, Joe Luft and Harry Ingham, put these categories of information together, and then put their first names together, to form what they called the *Johari Window*. [2]

With this as a model, many questions can be raised, and using in-

	Known to Self	Unknown to Self
Known to Others	I Open (Shared)	II Hidden (Denied)
Unknown to Others	III Blind (Repressed)	IV Unknown

[2] Reprinted from *Of Human Interaction*, by Joseph Luft, by permission of Mayfield Publishing Company (formerly National Press Books). Copyright © 1969 Joseph Luft.

terviews or questionnaires, some answers can be put forth. How much and what kind of information about oneself does a particular person wish to disclose? How much and what kind of information about others do we want to know? Because some of the frames of the window will be more filled with information than others, we may find correlations between the amount of information known and certain personality types or communication styles.

Even in the Johari window, however, things are not very complicated. That is, the "known to self" and "known to others" is no more complicated than the Xyx or the Yxy of our earlier model—what I think you think about me and *vice versa*. Logically, we could extend this much further: what I think you think I think you think I think you think about me. Roland D. Laing, a noted British psychoanalyst who has tried to see the bright side of mental illness, wrote an extraordinary little book called *Knots* in which he plays psychopoetic fugues upon such themes: [3]

Jack thinks
   he does not know
  what he thinks
   Jill thinks
   he does not know

But Jill thinks Jack does know it.

So Jill does not know
   she does not know
  that Jack does not know
  that Jill thinks
  that Jack does not know
and Jack does not know he does not know
  that Jill does not know she does not know
  that Jack does not know
   that Jill thinks Jack knows
what Jack thinks he does not know

That sort of extension may be much too involved for most of our ordinary interpersonal relationships, but in special cases—in some love affairs, sometimes in playing poker or bridge, or in some Byzan-

[3] R. D. Laing, *Knots* (New York: Pantheon Books, 1971), p. 59.

tine intrigues of espionage or diplomatic engagements—we might have to extend the perceptions of perceptions of perceptions for quite some distance.

Human relationships, even in everyday interpersonal communication, can be complicated. We do not want to overcomplicate things, but the greater danger may lie in oversimplification. For now, recognize that the idea of independent people communicating, the *I* and the *you*, is certainly oversimplified. You help to create my me, and yet *my* me is never quite the same as *your* me. And if I think about *your* me, then *my* me may not even be my first *your* me. But . . . well, you get the idea.

Pronouns Are Relative

The language of interpersonal communication is, to some extent, a language of personal pronouns. Personal pronouns, we may have been taught, take the place of personal nouns and are conventionally identified by singular or plural and by number, first, second, and third. Linguists tell us that the pronouns in any language can be fitted, with some squeezing or some stretching, into these six positions. In English, for example, we have:

	Singular	*Plural*
First person	I	we
Second person	you	you
Third person	he, she, it	they

We once used another form, "thou," as a more personal "you," but this has mostly disappeared from use except by some religious sects, such as the Quakers, or when quoting the King James version of the Bible, or singing old church hymns, or when writing bad poetry. If you have studied or happen to speak another language, such as Spanish, French, or German, you know that you have a choice of two words equivalent to the English "you"—*tu, usted; tu, vous; du, sie*—depending on whether the "you" is a good friend or relative, or a stranger or acquaintance on a formal occasion. Knowing when to switch from the formal to the familiar pronoun is a critical moment in interpersonal communication in these languages. Perhaps the closest we come is switching from a last name and title to a given name—"Don't call me Mr. Brown, call me Harry."

Some languages, however, are even more complicated in the array and arrangement of pronouns. The speaker of Japanese may choose among ten or more pronouns equivalent to the English "I," and about the same number for the equivalent of "you." Every choice reflects and implies some relationship between the "I" and the "you." Some of the pronouns are used to show an "I" of a subordinate status. Some show varying degrees of politeness, of respect, of formality and informality. Some are used only by women, some by men, some mainly by older people, some mainly by younger people. In short, the speaker of Japanese (and we could give examples from other languages as well) indicates through pronouns and other speech characteristics his or her perception of the particular human relationship. There is no exact equivalent to "I" or "you" as independent pronouns.

Put another way, in speaking English *I* am "I," no matter who *you* are, and *you* are "you," no matter who I am. In our relationship as identified by personal pronouns, *you* and *I* are *independent*. In Japanese, however, "our" relationship is always interdependent: one can scarcely say "How are you?" without guessing or knowing something about the other person in relationship to the speaker. A language is a part of a culture; we are born into both simultaneously and influenced by both. We must be careful not to say that a Japanese is more conscious of status, rank, and formality merely *because* of his language, or that a native English speaker is more individualistic and independent merely because of the English language, for there are many other influences from the culture. Nevertheless, language exerts some influence in interpersonal relationships, and thus we must be careful not to extend characteristics that may be true of many North Americans to people everywhere. Also we should not be surprised if a description or theory of interpersonal communication based on the American experience differs, possibly to a considerable extent, from a description made by a person from a different culture.

In any case, it is a gross distortion to regard two people in a conversation as totally independent, in the way that some diagrams of "person A" and "person B," or "listener" and "speaker" seem to suggest. It is better to emphasize *relationships*, and within any relationship note the point of focus: an "I-focused relationship," a "you-focused relationship," and forms of "we relationships."

An Eye for an I

A Greek student in the United States once remarked to his professor that English was the only language that used a capital letter for the first person singular pronoun—the "big I." The "capital self," Edward Stewart has called it.[4] For that student the big I symbolized much about American styles of communication, including independence, and individualism.

Apart from the history of the orthography of the first person pronoun, the independent and individualistic concept of "I" is worth further speculation. Some writers have noted that Western psychological thought has been generally I-focused. Freud theorized about the ego, superego, and the id. The ego was the self; the superego, a kind of overseer of the self, "an eye for an I." But in Freudian theory there is no "you" in the human equation.

Who am I? Sometimes my "me" seems to be of my own making; a person has some experience that he or she reduces to a self-description, often judgmental: "I'm no good at math." "I can't make it with girls." "I'm awkward." "I'm smarter than other kids." But more often, my "me" is not of my own making. Who I think I am has been distilled from countless experiences with others and what they have told me I am, or what I should be or what I must not be. Some of these labels are personal, some about my type. I may be told, that I:

————always wait until the last minute.
————am just like my father.
————am very pretty. My sister is the smart one.

I may be given advice on how to get on in this world:

[4] Edward C. Stewart, *American Cultural Patterns: A Cross-Cultural Perspective* (Pittsburgh: Regional Council for International Education, 1971), pp. 82–85.

Nice girls don't do that.

It's not what you know, it's who you know.

Men are all alike—they're only after one thing.

Then there are the vicarious experiences, ego trips, moments of fantasy or fleeting joy or pain that later form points of reference or standards that remain unattainable. That wonderful summer, that horrible party, that one time when the family was all together and really happy, that time when you were the star.

The meanings of experiences are ultimately personal meanings. Often the most off-hand remark by another makes a special impact. A simple statement can create waves of influence on the self that affect other for many years.

In every society, the dominant values will influence self-concepts just as they influence so many other aspects of communication. One's society teaches one to be independent or subordinate one's own feelings and work with the group; stand up and be counted, or, don't stand out or you will be pounded down. Compete, achieve, succeed; or, bend with the winds of times. The culture's stock of "models" for behavior seems endless: nursery rhymes and fairy tales, simple examples in school textbooks, popular songs and films, stories of great heroes and heroines, toys (doctors kits for boys, nurses kits for girls), and old sayings and folk logic. The impact is cumulative.

A mother wants to be independent. Day care centers and baby sitters help a bit; a separate room for the child helps; a bottle instead of the breast, the TV set instead of a mother's lullaby, these help. And in the process, the child learns the value of independence and will grow up wanting independence, too. Another society values some forms of dependence or interdependence. There, the baby is carried wherever the mother goes, the baby sleeps alongside the mother until the child is three or four years old; the mother anticipates the child's every need and satisfies it before the child needs to verbally express it through crying or calling. The neighbors will criticize the mother who does not. These are two styles that have subtle, but pervasive influences on the child's later sense of self and also on more apparent aspects of interpersonal communication. [5]

[5] See "Are Basic Needs Ultimate?" in Dorothy Lee, *Freedom and Culture* (Englewood Cliffs: Prentice-Hall, 1959), 70–77.

Egocentrics and Ethos

Literally, an I-focused style of communication is egocentric, a term with a selfish, negative nuance. There are popular notions about what sorts of people talk about themselves more than others—the famous or important are assumed to be self-centered, so that there is often much made of an important person who seems not to be egocentric.[6] The old joke about the movie star and his fan is illustrative: "Well," says the star after many minutes of talking about his great performances, "we've talked enough about me and my movies. Let's talk about you. How did *you* like my last movie?"

Powerful people are thought to be egocentric—the tyrants, fearsome or petty. Children are, unfairly perhaps, accused of being more self-centered than adults, so that a sign of immaturity is self-centeredness, and a mark of maturity is being able to share, to get along with others. Saying "you're acting childish" often means "you are acting selfish or being self-centered." Boring conversationalists, senile old folks who lapse into lengthy stories of "When I was a kid . . ." are regarded as too self-centered. Autistic children who live in their own world and cannot relate to reality and other people who exhibit signs of mental illnesses are frequently characterized as self-centered. Such types are both reflections of communication and products of other communication. As types they also serve as models of communication behavior to avoid.

Victims or people suffering from personal losses may withdraw into themselves. Society tolerates this only for a time. If a person persists in feeling sorry for himself, acting with self-pity, for too long, others resent it. "You've got to find something outside of yourself," the friend may advise. As a society we may encourage such self-pity by avoiding the victim—the person whose husband or wife has died, the divorcee, the handicapped.[7] The social models of saints and heroes, of course,

---

[6] This seems to be but one example of the popularly expressed surprise when a person whose role is regarded as very special turns out to act in ways that are quite ordinary. The very wealthy, the clergy, and even politicians occasionally inspire naïve amazement when they do very ordinary things. When Gerald Ford was first installed in the office as president, dozens of articles and editorials were written about his choosing to make his own breakfast.

[7] For a fascinating treatise on the public treatment of people who are seen as tainted or defective in some socially identified way, see Erving Goffman, *Stigma* (Englewood Cliffs, N.J.: Prentice-Hall, 1963).

are those who seem to care more for others than for themselves, who despite their suffering, pain, handicap, whatever, seek to serve others. And then the irony: the selfish man, having become a hero, is suddenly praised as so important that he becomes self-centered!

It is interesting that although an I-focused style of communication is discredited, it remains the norm at the level of the sentence (in English). More sentences begin with "I" than with any of the other pronouns. This point is more obvious in writing than in speech—glance at any recent personal letter. Commercial letters, particularly advertising promotions, tend to avoid the "I" and stress the "you."

It is interesting to compare the I-centered style with what Aristotle called the *ethos* of a persuasive speaker. In the classical view of how people are persuaded—a view that has been generally validated through contemporary empirical research—the most important fact was not the speaker's rational appeals (*logos*) or his emotional appeals (*pathos*), but rather those qualities that the speaker evinced about himself; his character, competence, and good will. In short, if the audience trusted the speaker, the speaker was more than half way there in persuading them. And so the good persuader had to learn how to boost himself, to influence what the audience felt about him (or her, though Aristotle gives almost no mention of women persuaders). The would-be persuader must seem to be all of the things he would like to say he is, but must say them without alienating his listeners. Thus a very I-centered person must do his best not to appear to be so. To be thought wise, one must never say, "I am wise". To be thought brave, one must never say, "I am brave." To be thought modest, one must never say, "I am modest."

In stressing the importance of the speaker's *ethos*, Aristotle introduced an extremely astute observation—one's *ethos* pervades other identifiable aspects of communication. That is, Aristotle associated the *ethos* with the speaker as a person. The *pathos* or emotional appeals, he associated with the listeners or audience; the *logos*, with the substance of the speech itself. None of these was regarded as totally independent. It was the *ethos* that largely influenced the other two but, apparently, not usually the other way around. If you trust and respect a speaker then the emotional appeal seems sincere, the logical evidence seems convincing. If you do not trust the speaker then these appeals may seem hollow and unconvincing.

What Aristotle described for formal, public forms of communication seems equally applicable to the more familiar, everyday experiences of interpersonal communication. The "I"—or at least how others regard that "I"—pervades all that he or she talks about. Whenever "I" talks there is, by implication if not intention, some information about the speaker as well as the subject. "You have a lovely dress," may say something nice about the dress and its wearer; it may also indicate that the speaker is perceptive, has good taste in clothing, or even—if the wearer really thinks it is a terrible dress—that the speaker lacks taste. For one person to say to another, "You are right!" may imply that (a) the speaker is intelligent enough to recognize that the other is right, or (b) is slow to discover that. And, as we will see shortly, such statements also express aspects of a relationship between the "I" and the "You," as well as the information about each person. "Your work is excellent," may be said by a grade school teacher to his or her pupil, but it is not so often said by a student to the teacher.

In broader and more subtle ways, almost anything said by one person about another includes a great deal of information about the speaker as well: the choice of words, formal or slangy; the tone of voice, confident or tense; even the choice of commenting on a subject in the first place.

You Are My Destiny

If "I" is the pronoun that is heard most frequently in our prosaic conversations every day, then it would seem it is the "you" that most often appears in poetry and song—particularly in love songs. Count the frequency of "you" in the titles and first words of today's top ten hits. And similarly, if "I" likes to talk of "I," it also seems that when it comes to listening, "I" likes most to hear the magic word "you."

There are many popular soppy songs that say that *without you* there would be no sun, no stars, and so on. We might dismiss these as the excesses of a young person in love. But serious writers have said something even more startling: *without you* there would be no *I* (or me). Back in the days when the division between the humanities and social sciences was not so sharply defined, America produced several brilliant theorists whose ideas continue to be influential today. One was George Herbert Mead. Mead's theories of "the significant gesture" and "the significant symbol" continue to attract and inform us today; and it seems especially relevant to the 'I" and the "you." [8] For Mead, the onset of human communication, of language, and of self-awareness lies in the ability of an individual to vicariously identify with the other to the extent that the speaker was aware of the effect that a gesture or a verbal expression would create for the listener. Mead, who at the time was strongly influenced by the theories of Charles Darwin and the evolutionary development from animals to humans, began by examining what happens when two animals, such as two dogs, meet each other. They might circle each other, sniff each other, growl, or fight. This may or may not be called communication, but to Mead it was at least quite different from human behavior, because each dog was only reacting to the behavior of the other dog. It was a pattern of action and reaction. When a dog snarls at another dog, it does not imagine how that other dog might react to the snarl. But when a human snarls at another human, the snarler can imagine himself being snarled at, know how he would react, and hence assume the reaction of the other. For Mead, animal-like gestures evolved into "significant gestures,"—that is, behavior that had meaning. "The significant gesture," in turn, evolved into a more sophisticated mode of expression, "the significant symbol," which marked the beginnings of language and human communication.

Mead's speculations may not be historically or even biologically accurate; much more is known today about brain differences between humans and animals and about language development. But his speculations are still provocative for they stress the importance of the "you" in the creation of a sense of "I." "I" needs "you." Without "you" there is no "me." This theme, and variations on it, will run through much of our exploration of interpersonal communication. Reactions to the word *you*, will depend very much on how that word is used: *you* are wonderful; *you* are disgusting; *you* are pregnant. Perhaps this would be less true if English had a richer repertoire of pronouns. In Japanese, for example, at least one of the *you* words is often used more or less as an English speaker might use the word darling or honey. Some Japa-

---

[8] George H. Mead, *Mind, Self and Society* (Chicago: University of Chicago Press, 1934), p. 135.

nese wives refer to their husbands only as *anata*, rarely using given names, while another word for you expresses utter contempt.

In English we can roughly distinguish between two styles of communication in which *you* appears to be the subject. One of these we may call directive and, later in the book, we will talk about "instrumental forms of communication," which are not so different. In this case, although you may be the subject, the aura of influence seems to emanate from the speaker: "You did it wrong." "You have done well." "*I* know what is right but you apparently don't," or "I approve of what you have done." The other style of communication appears to reduce the influence of the speaker; it may be called nondirective in some cases, and functionally it seems closer to affective communication, which we will also discuss later in the book. Both of these styles, not surprisingly, have been widely discussed and contrasted in the field of counseling, teaching, therapy, and other helping relationships.

Let Me Help You

Johnny has a problem, or so he says, or so somebody says. Somebody should talk to Johnny. We may find two possible forms of communication in that style of talking that illustrate and extend what we have said. One kind of person—Johnny's father or teacher or counselor—may be very directive: "See here, young man, you are doing such and such and if you keep it up this will result; the reason you are doing this is probably such and such; stop it; do that; or else." Although Johnny and his behavior seem to be the subject of the remarks, the implicit communication is very I-centered on the part of the person giving advice. He or she is saying, in effect, "I see through you. I know what is best. Do what I say." A Freudian therapist of the old school might use a similar approach, with the therapist forcing the patient to face up to a problem he refuses to acknowledge and often, in the process, transferring Johnny's troubling emotions to the therapist himself. Freud's society was one of authoritarian fathers, and one latter-day criticism of some aspects of Freudian theory is that although it applied well to a society like Vienna of the early part of this century, it is irrelevant today.

But our Johnny today may be more likely to meet a counselor or a parent who uses a different approach, a non-directive approach of the kind most identified with Carl Rogers (the Rogerian approach).[9] This is far more you-focused, with the role of the helper being to aid the person to see the problem for himself and resolve it for himself. A helper who is very supportive of the other is required in this approach, (in therapy, client-centered; in teaching, student-centered) so that the person with the problem feels free to face the problem and resolve it.

Rogerian techniques—and there are many such techniques—often involve little more than showing that the helper is a good, sympathetic listener. Indeed, the helper (counselor, therapist, friend, or relative) will do his or her best to express almost the same meaning, if not words, that the person with the problem has expressed. The helper's first goal is to show that he or she has really listened, understands, and wants to hear more without passing judgment. A typical pattern might be:

TROUBLED: I'm really frustrated.
HELPER: Really? You are having some problems?
TROUBLED: Yes, I don't know where I am going any more. I feel lost.
HELPER: You feel you lack direction. . . .

As the troubled person slowly reveals to the helper and thus to himself what the problem is, how he feels about it, and how he might cope with it, it is hoped that he can resolve it. The counselor seeks to avoid giving any advice or even any information—at least at this stage. The counselor succeeds by not trying to succeed. Technique alone, of course, does not always work, and Rogerian techniques used clumsily have been parodied:

TROUBLED: I got problems!
HELPER: You're having difficulties. . . .
TROUBLED: What's wrong with the way I said it?

A best-selling book on communication, *Between Parent and Child,* by Haim Ginott, similarly urged you-focused communication

[9] See Carl Rogers, *Client Centered Therapy* (Cambridge: Riverside Press, 1951).

on the part of the parents in communicating with their children.[10] A typical reaction to a child's request to stay up until 10:30 to watch a movie on TV might be: "No, you can't. You have to go to bed at 9:00." Again an I-focused response from the parent's point of view—*I give the orders around here.* Ginott urged empathy to demonstrate to the child that the parent heard, understood, and sympathized with the child. Similarly, if a child comes home sad about an experience at school, the wise parent should identify with the child before giving advice or even seeking more information.

CHILD: A terrible thing happened at school.
PARENT: You seem unhappy.
CHILD: Yeah, the teacher shouted at me because I didn't turn in a paper.
PARENT: You must have felt terrible.
CHILD: I sure did. In front of all the other kids, too.
PARENT: You probably felt like crying.
CHILD: Yeah, I did. . . . How did you know?

The parent and child explore these feelings and the problem together. Ginott indicates a four-step sequence:

1. The parent, recognizing the child's wish, expresses it simply: "You wish you could go to the movies tonight."
2. He clearly sets limits on a specific act: "Our rule is 'no movies on school nights.' "
3. He may show ways to, at least, partially satisfy the child's desire: "You may go to the movies on Friday or Saturday night."
4. He helps the child to express some of the resentment that is likely to arise when restrictions are imposed: "It is obvious that you don't like the rule. You wish there weren't such a rule. You wish the rule were every night is movie night. When you grow up and have your own home, you are sure going to change this rule." [11]

[10] Haim Ginott, *Between Parent and Child* (New York: Macmillan, 1965).
[11] Ibid, p. 33.

There are, however, some limitations and even some possible risks, in the approach that Ginott advocates. As mentioned earlier, the line between analysis and projection is thin indeed, and it is possible that when parents think they have figured out what the child is thinking, the parents may actually be projecting their own feelings and assumptions, which might complicate some problems. And even if the parent were able to always get inside the head of the child and verbalize the child's thoughts and feelings, one wonders what long-range effect that might have on the child's later view of parents himself, and of the process of communication.

With some caution, we can relate the kinds of communication described previously as I-focused and you-focused, directive and nondirective, to two categories often used in distinguishing among functions of communication, the affective and the instrumental. However, any one form of expression may serve several different functions, even for the same persons in the same situations, Although there may be advantages in relating the you-focus to the affective and the I-focus to the instrumental, we should not ignore other applications.

Affective Communication

Affective communication is characterized by a you-focused expression of feelings or emotions. Because the word *emotion* is a vague term and both intended or actual arousal of emotions in another person is difficult to ascertain, we must be careful in freely using the functional category of affective communication. [12] Expressions of praise, both sincere and brazen flattery, as well as expressions of criticism, are among the most common forms. Note that while we have spoken of a you-focus, it is also possible for a speaker to praise or criticize himself or

[12] Writers in this field often mention affective language as well as an affective function of communication. In some languages, as in Spanish, certain word forms, such as diminutives, are most associated with affective speech; in English where diminutives are less apparent and serve somewhat different functions, the equivalents would include words like "cute little . . . ," or "little old . . . ," or certain rhyming or repetitive forms, e.g., palsy-walsy, buddy-buddy, that's a no-no. Perhaps these are most associated with child-like or female speech and, regionally, with southern and southwestern speech.

herself as well, but in this case the self often seems to be treated as a separate entity.

As with other functional interpretations, words intended as affective may be interpreted differently by the listener, and vice versa; and, of course, the affective may be only a part of or a means to other functions, particularly the instrumental function. Also, along with the instrumental, affective functions are probably the most associated with certain role behaviors. Thus it is not surprising that if "the Southern belle" is a model of a user of affective language, she is—in a stereotype, at least—a model of role behavior ascribed to being "feminine," to be gentle, "charming," and never appear to compete with or contradict "a gentleman." Such a role, which may already have largely disappeared in the South, is still the norm in many other societies throughout the world. It is also closely related to the complementary relationship pattern that seems so much more widespread than American values that favor symmetrical relationships.

As we have already suggested, persons in subordinate positions may have to rely largely on affective language to achieve instrumental goals in communication with superiors. Indeed, to identify who uses what kind of language toward which people is one of the clearest tests of status, rank and power.

Instrumental Communication

Instrumental communication in its most blatant form is an expression of command. Do this. Stop that. Come here. Sometimes, as in some jobs, instrumental commands are expressed in very stark forms, but often such direct expressions may seem too bossy or seem to indicate anger. Thus "please" or "would you mind?" may be used to soften the tone. Perhaps as a general rule, the higher a person's rank or status and the clearer one's role of authority, the more likely the person is to use direct instrumental language. In the United States, and perhaps generally, the instrumental style is more associated with male speech than female speech and is more frequent in communication among people of the same sex, and similar ages and backgrounds, than in mixed groups. We should also expect more instrumental language in private than in front of strangers, unless part of one's public performance requires a dramatization of authority command, such as an army sergeant, a football quarterback, or a traffic cop.

Scholars who have been attracted by learning theory or some variant of the stimulus-response or reward-punishment view of how behavior operates may wish to view nearly all communication as essentially instrumental. This seems too generalized, however, at least if we wish to make finer discriminations in style and purpose of communication. That is, saying "ouch," or "how do you do?" or making a joke may each influence some later action, but to regard all such expressions as primarily instrumental seems to overextend the function.

We seem to have little respect for a person who seems to overuse the affective language of praise toward another; one may be called a yes-man, a flatterer, a sychophant, or an ass-kisser, and yet, as many have remarked over the years, flattery seems least obvious to the person being flattered.

History and literature provide us with many dramatic examples of the powerful, highly I-centered, instrumentally styled superior who maintains a retinue of yes-men, people who never disagree, never express doubts, never ever use instrumental commands in return to their superior. It is interesting that the people who do provide criticism seem to be outsiders, such as the soothsayer warning Caesar, or journalists and opposition leaders warning a president. The political lesson of this pattern in the extreme is that the top man—the Caesar, the president—becomes cut off from vital information and criticism until eventually events overtake the flattery of the yes-men. History and drama, too, provide us with revelations about the flatterer who in the end turns out to be far less loyal and sincere than his old boss had ever suspected.

The logic of grammar indicates that the first person singular (I) combines with the second person singular (you) to make first person plural, as if "we" were you and I, but especially I. "We" may or may not include my perception of you; in some cases "we" might not even include another person. Consider Charles Lindberg. Lindberg was the first person to fly alone across the Atlantic Ocean. Actually he did not fly alone. He flew in an airplane. He wrote a book about this, a book called *We*, meaning he and his plane. The plane was not a mere object for him; it became personified, it deserved equal credit.

Some drivers also personify their cars, sailors their ships, and some horseback riders talk to their horses. It is possible to have some sort of a "we" relationship even when one is alone.

But usually "we" means two or more people who have something in common, or, better, who recognize or emphasize something in common. Among the oldest techniques of persuasion, as in political persuasion, is to stress some "we" relationship between speaker and audience. This technique is often called common ground. Kenneth Burke, who we will discuss at greater length later, said that the basis of all persuasion is that "we" relationship, what he calls identification.

The "we," however, often has little meaning apart from "they." Sometimes what makes us "we" is mostly that we are not like "them." It is sometimes supposed that one thing that will give a "we" feeling to all of humanity is a threat from something inhuman—creatures from outer space. Then it will be "we" people against "them."

What we share may be outward behavior—the language we speak, the style of clothing we wear, the dances we dance. A sense of "we" may be less noticeable, i.e., our religious beliefs or political philosophies. "We" at times may include millions of others we have never seen and never will see: the *consciousness* movements of "we Blacks," "we women," or "we members of the third world." The feeling of "we" may be as intimate and inviolable as the relationship between lovers, or brothers and sisters, fathers and sons, celebrated in the great legends and literature of the world. Or "we" may be exploited, commercialized as in advertising appeals to create a sense of identification with some product; such as "the Pepsi generation." Of these pronouns the "*we*" is both the vaguest, most fluctuating, and yet the most essential in considering interpersonal communication.

In a very broad sense, communication involves a shifting focus between identification and detachment, an interplay among "I" and "you" and "we." The two people at the corner may give scant notice to one another unless there is an accident; then, "we must do something!" Even if these two would seem to have nothing else in common—of different ages, perhaps even coming from different countries, and not speaking a common language—at that moment there is a sense of "we." Or at the other extreme, a boy and his father may have a very close relationship for many years, but as the boy begins to identify more with others of his age, he may feel as if his father has become a stranger to him. The common language seems unimportant when compared to the differences in the use of slang, in jokes, and in recognition of "what's happening."

In some ways human relations resemble the process of the cell that divides, combines agains, and through such successive detachment and combining evolves and grows. Who you would identify with now is not who you identified with before nor, probably, who you will identify with even five years from now.

Two Kinds of Reference Groups

In describing communication it is sometimes convenient to speak of reference groups, those people, real or imagined, who serve to give us considerable guidance for our actions. We should consider two kinds of reference groups: those groups with which we identify, the "we" groups, and those that we compare ourselves with or distinguish ourselves from, the "they" groups. These two kinds of groups are not fixed and stable, however. The cross-town high school or rival college may be "they" at an annual football game; but both may form a "we" group for an all-city team or in some demands of student rights, as opposed to "they," the authorities, or the Board of Education. It is also apparent that any person may be grouped with others in ways that the individual may not have thought of or even approve of. The foreign students, for example, may come to feel a "we" relationship that none had ever felt before; indeed students who in their own countries might feel strongly in opposition to students from some other country may come to feel or at least be treated as having something in common. And it is true that prejudice often asserts itself in the form of shifts in "we-they" reference groups. Some Jewish scholars have remarked that a "Jewish identity" might have disappeared or have been greatly diminished over the years if the Jews had not been treated as a group and ostracized. Racial discrimination in the United States, of course, has been a result of a pervasive white "we" relationship from which "they," the blacks were distinguished. Which in turn yielded black consciousness, black pride, and the evolving salient symbols of soul.[13]

[13] There is no comparable black consciousness in Brazil, where assimilation rather than exclusion has been the historical rule.

Women's consciousness seems to have followed much the same pattern, and indeed there is no reason why any group which is or which imagines itself as excluded from some other "we" could not evolve its own sense of identification. Finally, for now, we should note that one of the clearest expressions of exclusion or prejudice occurs when an individual is treated as if he or she represents an entire reference group.

The Language of "We": Ritual

About a decade ago a massive blizzard socked in Chicago's O'Hare International Airport, stranding thousands of passengers for days. Having nothing to do and no place to go, many strangers struck up friendships and came to know each other very well. And each year, for many years afterward, one group would hold an annual reunion—at the airport.

Shared experiences often lead us to desire a celebration of the sharing: a cast party at the end of the dramatic performances, class reunions, homecoming parties, and indeed parties to celebrate almost any endeavor that has emotionally bound people together over a period of time. Some philosophers see this human need as the basis of religion—the celebration of the sharing, of oneness.

These clebrations in time become rituals, expressing a we-feeling in the language of "we." A ritual celebrates not only a sense of community but also a sense of continuity, of timelessness, of things that do not change while so much else is changing. Few symbols have such a powerful evocative effect as the symbols of ritual, particularly when the ritual is still bound to experiences. Ritual that evokes only ritual is a dying one.

There are many languages of ritual—not just words and songs but also smells (of incense, candles), tastes (of special foods prepared for the occasion), of weather associated with the event that is celebrated. Even commercialization can become grafted onto some rituals. The logic is of association and recollection or evocation.

One reason the ritual language of "we" relations is especially strong is that it discourages a distinction between "I" and "you." Songs, so much a part of any ritual, are sung together; arms are linked. Bodies sway as a single great wave: *"We shall overcome."* And so while rituals evoke past, shared experiences, they also impress upon the participants a sense of "we" for present or future efforts. [14]

Most of what are recognized as rituals are also characterized by repetition of words in which the verbal form is functionally more important than the referents for the words. Words may be in Latin, or Greek, or Middle English and may have little specific meaning for the person who speaks the words; the meaning is the "we" sense of repeating these with others and particularly the "we" of the past—our ancestors or our childhood memories. Perhaps when reciting The Pledge of Allegiance or The Lord's Prayer most American children do not know what some of those words mean, but by learning the form, the sound of the words, a sense of "we" is established. Thus group chanting or singing is an ideal ritual expression—the "we" is enhanced by everybody talking at once. Initiations into groups, even those in which everybody talks brotherhood or sisterhood (the family metaphor is significant) often involve a certain degree of pain and humiliation particularly during a designated period (hell week). Every campus has its own legendary exploits—pledges fed a sumptuous dinner secretly laced with a strong laxative, then chained together and taken as a group to a movie—with predictable results. Along with such nonsense is imparted other information, perhaps equally nonsensical but endowed with arcane symbolism; and most of these—secret handshakes, code words, promises of undying loyalty, and the like—behaviors are clearly communicative expressions. [15]

Nearly every group that considers itself a group is likely to have some calculated behavior that tests, informs, and admits the younger or newer member into the established community. The form, the

---

[14] In the U.S., the suicide rate jumps dramatically during the Christmas season—apparently because while we are exhorted to be merry and with our loved ones, many unfortunate people face a reality which is lonely and anything but merry; the contrast at this season is too painful for some to endure.

[15] Anthropologists have often likened these activities to more serious puberty rites in other societies in which the young men or young women of the tribe officially pass into adult status in the community. Circumcision rites for men are among the most widespread examples of a part of such a rite; a boy becomes a man. These usually are performed for an age group, not individually, to mark the passage from childhood to manhood as a group; and in the process to increase the bonds of identification within that group.

degree of humiliation and pain, and the degree of secrecy or openness may differ, but functionally the ceremonies are remarkably similar.

Symmetrical and Complementary Relationships

A very useful distinction between kinds of interpersonal relationships is that of symmetrical and complementary relations. The distinction is a simple one. Symmetrical relationships are based on an assumption of likeness, or similarity; complementary relationships are based on assumptions of differences, which complement each other to make a whole. Neither kind of relationship is necessarily better or worse than the other, and all of us are likely to participate in each without giving too much thought to such a distinction.

Some examples may help to distinguish the two. In baseball, the relationship between a pitcher and a catcher is complementary; the catcher cannot be a catcher without a pitcher, and the pitcher cannot be a pitcher without a catcher. Together they form one whole unit.[16] Pitchers may be more famous, catchers may be better hitters, but that is another matter. In their relationship they need each other, and their differences are thus valued. We do not criticize the catcher because he cannot pitch, or criticize the pitcher because he is not a good catcher. Because outfielders have a much more symmetrical relationship, they can be moved around; we would criticize a right fielder who said he was not good at playing left field.

Doctors and nurses usually have a complementary relationship. There may be an assumption among some doctors that any old doctor could be a nurse but not even the best nurse could be a doctor, but in their professional duties they are expected to complement each other, to work together to make a complete whole. What of husbands and wives? In the past in the United States and predominantly throughout the world still, the relationship was complementary. Husbands were breadwinners, credited with the ability to do hard physical work, the final authority, the voice of reason. Wives were to stay at home, clean, cook, bear children and take care of them. Women were the weaker sex, second in command to men, and said to be more emo-

---

[16] Thus the name *the battery*.

tional. Some things have changed. Most of what is called work today requires relatively little physical labor and in any case can be performed as well by women as by men. Mutually accepted mythologies about the nature of men and women have greatly disappeared, or at least changed. Children have become financially more of a liability than an asset (not so many hands needed down on the farm these days), and the promises of sexual equality have been tested at the bar of justice. Today, husband-wife relationships in the United States are far more likely to be symmetrical, based on similarities of interest, education, and so on. Except for bearing children, father and mother are interchangeable. But imagine a nation in which tradition emphasizes and values expressed differences between the sexes; where women speak a language that is noticeably different from men, where a man's word almost always counts for more than a woman's, where a woman will keep her opinion to herself if it should differ from that of a man. There are many such cultures. Probably most of the world is closer to this pattern than the pattern described for the United States. Male-female relationships, including marriages, in such cultures reflect complementary relationships.

In Japan, which might be described above, there are other aspects of complementary relationships; relative age is very important, so that the younger person will nearly always defer to the older, while the older person bears responsibility for the younger person. Differences in status, too, are emphasized. For good communication one must always know if the other person is of superior or subordinate rank; titles and honorifics are used generously to express and maintain these differences.

As a culture, Americans place great value on symmetrical relationships, minimizing differences that might suggest inequality. Americans tend not to like titles or honorifics that suggest some superior/subordinate relationship. There are professors, politicians, more than a handful of college presidents, and apparently a very large number of fathers who like to be called by their first names. "Don't think of me as your dad, I want to be your buddy." Some wives now refuse to take the names of their husbands because that proposition seems asymmetrical. "If he won't take my name, why should I take his?" There are other evidences of the value placed on equality leading to symmetrical relationships—distrust of authority, support of the underdog, a love of games in which by rule all players start out as equals. The political counterpart of this is that anybody born in America can win the race for the presidency.

Symmetrical relationships maximize similarities of age, sex, role, or status and serve to encourage the apparent differences of each individual as an individual. "I will treat you as you treat me and then we can each be ourselves," is a statement of the basis of the symmetrical relationships. Complementary relationships maximize differences in age, sex, role, or status and serve to encourage the mutuality of the relationship, the interdependence.

There are tensions in each of these realtionships. In a symmetrical relationship, a modern American marriage, or open marriage let us say, there is a constant risk that one party will feel that the other is not doing an equal share of the work or has a larger share of privileges and so on. The wife may complain that the husband never does his share of the chores around the house; or the husband may complain that he does his share of the house work, but the wife isn't contributing a fair share of the income. If one person seems too uppity, the other may either try to put that one down or seek for a balance by also becoming uppity. In a system based on the value of equality there is always the fear that, in Orwell's celebrated phrase from *Animal Farm*, some will be "more equal than others." A level balance is most difficult to maintain. And if things get too bad, the "we" may split into "you" and "I."

In some respects a complementary relationship is easier to maintain—so long as both (and also outsiders, for their view of things may actually be more important for the feelings of each in the relationship)—adhere to the values of such a relationship. It has been observed, for example, that in societies where the cultural values assert male superiority in various forms, it is actually easier for the wife to be bossy. The man can take it for he knows that he is a man and thus the real boss. Moreover, if a complementary relationship such as a conventional marriage is rigidly enforced by social custom and values, there will be fewer opportunities for the two parties to invade each other's domain and threaten the relationship. The husband will never enter the kitchen and may not even be home as much as in a society where symmetrical relationships are valued. The wife will grow up valuing her role as mother and homemaker and feel herself as incomplete or unfulfilled if she has not undertaken these roles. This sort of notion may sound terribly reactionary and sexist in the United States today, so let me assure you that I am not advocating this for the United States but merely trying to point out that this is the kind of marriage relationship that is the most common historically and throughout the world today, and not all women in such situations are just waiting to be liberated. When cultural values do change, often from the most innocuous beginnings, and when people are not satisfied with certain kinds of complementary relationships, then the value system fails and some new form must be found. In the United States in the 1960s and 1970s, it appears that there was such a shift in values: we saw Black Power, Women's Lib., Student Power . . . and Red Power, Brown Power, Youth Power, and Old People's Power. These power or consciousness movements, however, may not have represented radical changes in American values so much as demands for legal and social support for the constitutional guarantee that all men (presumably to be amended to read "all persons") are created equal. The U.S. Constitution seems to clearly assert the value of symmetrical, not complementary, human relationships.

But values are not always the same as actual behavior, and even if Americans would seem to be more comfortable with symmetrical relationships, there is probably no American who does not experience and value at least some complementary relations. We will return to this theme and distinction throughout this book. To speak of interpersonal relations or of "we" relations is much too general to describe the ways in which we relate to others, expect certain behaviors of them, and in turn are expected to behave.

Third Persons

For the existentialist philosopher and writer Jean Paul Sartre, an existentialist hell is "other people." Sartre's famous play, No Exit, is a vision of hell populated by three people.[17] What makes Sartre's hell is the combination of individuals whose weaknesses are constantly exposed to and by each other, and from which there is no escape.

[17] The choice of three seems especially significant; relationships among three people seem more problematic than relationships between two or among four or five.

The hell on earth for many people must surely be an involvement in a situation that is devoid of sympathy or empathy, where one's weaknesses and frustrations are constantly exposed and made to fester. Hell may be other people—he, she, they—but not so often you. We seem to do our best to avoid communicating with people we do not like so that they appear in reality or in imagination as third persons or vaguely defined forces—the establishment, the system. And feelings of hate or envy, directed toward some third persons, are, it is often said, self-consuming. It has been observed that people who must refer to third persons whom they fear or even hate will use euphemisms like "that man" or circumlocutions ("you know who") to symbolically distance the person still further. In the paranoid style "he" or "she" becomes "they," and "they" are everywhere. In this grim picture of hell, third persons become a basic reference group against whom much communication is directed or evaluated. Scapegoats, those people who are blamed for our problems, are third persons or comparable, impersonal forces. Where hate is strongest, even the sense of person is lost and "they" become animals, insects, monsters, and their destruction further impersonalized. In Hitler's state, the Jews were officially symbolized as vermin, and their destruction euphemized as the final solution. In the official reporting of the Vietnam war, the enemy was transformed into the statistic of a body count. Since it seems that most of these "counts" had little or no basis in reality, presumably the major function was to depersonify people.

If we sometimes have the feeling that hell is other people who get in our way, prevent us from becoming or at least imagining who we want to be, it is also true that some third persons are charged with responsibility for doing precisely the opposite—facilitating communication. As we will see later, Americans at the level of cultural values encourage directness of communication. As children we learn of Miles Standish's irreparable mistake in sending John Alden to woo Priscilla: "Speak for yourself, John," she said, and John spoke and Miles was out. "Tell it like it is," "let it all hang out," "level with me." We have had many such urgings to be direct. But not all societies or even all elements of American society are like this. Indeed, it appears that the value of directness is rather unusual in the world. Rather, the use of third persons as mediators, interlocutors, or go-betweens is widespread. Today some writers identify these as buffers, or gatekeepers, people who stand between and moderate the messages passing between "I" and "you" or the two principle parties.

School children sometimes involve go-betweens in adolescent romances. Bobby is too shy to tell Mary that he likes her a lot, so he gets Freddy or Lulu to tell Mary and then to report back. This saves Bobby and Mary embarrassment, particularly if Mary thinks Bobby is a boob. On a somewhat more sophisticated level a person like the president's news secretary also serves this role. It is easier for reporters to ask the secretary direct questions than to ask the president, and easier for the news secretary to say "I don't know," "I'll find out," or other equivocations than for the president to seem unsure or uninformed. Front people of all kinds—particularly secretaries—serve a similar role.

Gerry Phillipsen, in his fascinating study of Chicago's back-of-the yards area, describes his surprise in seeing highly verbal, young men apply for some job opening.[18] He reports that they would often stand in the corner of the office while a third party spoke for them. Clearly, John was not to speak for himself.

There are also third persons who do not participate in communication directly, but who observe and report to those who are communicating, much as referees or scorekeepers serve in games or judges in a court of law.

It is the responsibility and risk of such a go-between to appear to be neutral or, perhaps even more likely, as Goffman has noted, to appear to be more loyal to one side when talking to that person, and more loyal to the other when talking to the other person.[19] It is often a frustrating responsibility.

Some go-between roles that were once instrumental have become more ritualistic over the years, such as the bridesmaid or the best man. But other roles for go-betweens have increased as society seems to become more complex and specialized: employment agents, parole officers, family counselors, welfare social workers. Much of the training for such specialized roles is chiefly in interpersonal communication.

In a traditional society no less than in the small, small world of a

[18] Gerry Phillipsen, "Speaking 'Like a Man' in Teamsterville: Culture Patterns of Role Enactment in an Urban Neighborhood," *The Quarterly Journal of Speech*, 61: 1, Feb. 1975), p. 20.

[19] Erving Goffman, *The Presentation of Self in Everyday Life* Garden City: Doubleday Anchor, 1959).

grade school classroom, the people who serve as go-betweens and messengers are usually those personally known by the people they would serve. Even a very experienced matchmaker with dozens of successful matches to her or his credit will still enter into a personal relationship with each prospective match. And should the marriage later experience problems, it is the matchmaker's duty to try to help resolve the problem. The traditional matchmaker was at least a he or a she (and in communication a "you") and never a "they" or an "it." This is a far cry from computer dating bureaus.

What seems to have happened in society over the years is that functions of communication that once could be performed by identifiable people, most often friends, are increasingly performed by unknown people somewhere down the line. The bureaucracies, so often devised to serve specialized functions of interpersonal communication, provide, as Franz Kafka anticipated a century ago, impersonal communication.

Summary

Human relationships are more complex than our simple perceptions and language categories might indicate. Even when only two people meet and converse, each has several perceptions of himself and of the other person, and the process of communication both reflects and influences these. Our perceptions of ourselves are in part the product of past encounters with others and may have been influenced by particular labels applied by others in very different situations. Society further offers general guidelines of how an individual might and even should regard himself or herself in its attention to differences of sex, relative age, marital status, and the like.

We have suggested several ways of viewing interpersonal communication in specific relationships. An I-focused relationship shows some parallel to instrumental communication, including requests and commands; a you-focused relationship may favor more affective or emotive forms of communication, including compliments and flattery directed toward the other's emotions. We have also noted some parallel between these and forms of teaching and counseling, the former more directive, the latter more nondirective or client centered.

Furthermore, individuals identify with others who seem to share common interests, and backgrounds, while at the same time being aware of still other groups of persons with whom they consciously do not identify. Both of these reference groups help to shape one's self-concept and also influence with whom one talks, how one talks, and about what one talks.

When persons join together into a "we" relationship, much of their communication may be characterized by a ritual form. Rituals may serve in part to initiate a new member into a stable organization and to celebrate the oneness of the group. One of the dominant characteristics of ritual, as well as major function, is to provide a sense of timelessness or changelessness and hence a very high predictability of expressions. Although this quality serves the members' feeling of closeness, it also serves to emotionally separate those who are outside of the group. Hence any celebration of "we" implies the existence of "they."

Stable interpersonal relationships may be divided into two kinds, symmetrical and complementary. Symmetrical relationships are based on and emphasize similarities between the individuals, while minimizing any significant differences (such as differences in age or sex or status). Complementary relationships, in contrast, find their strength in valued differences between the parties; each person complements the other to form some complete whole. Although every person may identify relationships of each kind, there are also cultural influences that favor one kind or the other. Many interpretations of communication that have arisen in the United States tend to favor symmetrical relationships between equals.

There are also third parties who are neither "we" nor "they," but who may serve to initiate or facilitate interpersonal communication. These include contacts, go-betweens, and on occasion judges, counselors, or simply onlookers. Their roles tend to be essentially complementary, and their style of communication is frequently instrumental. Although many contemporary studies of interpersonal communication may relegate such third parties to a position in the background, their influence in interpersonal encounters cannot be ignored.

To try to clarify and illustrate some of the concepts and themes developed in these first two chapters, we will turn next to a brief passage from fiction, the popular novel *Love Story* by Erich Segal.

THREE
FOR EXAMPLE . . .

Here it may be helpful to illustrate some of what we have been considering thus far and also to anticipate much that we will discuss later. For this purpose we have chosen a brief excerpt from the popular novel of a few years back, *Love Story* by Erich Segal. Some justifications may be in order, not only for this particular choice but for the use of fiction in general.

The line between fiction and fact in presentations of conversation is not as precise as some might suppose. Attempt to report any conversation that you have overheard or even participated in and you will find that you omit most of the actual data of the interaction. Even if a full presentation of the verbal behavior is given, the treatment of all that is involved in communication is still incomplete. Moreover, you may have to add some explanation or interpretation of your own to make that conversation more meaningful to a third party. Thus you may have to add explanations of the relationship between the persons conversing, clarify the referents (for matters merely alluded to or implied), and possibly add some comments about events that led up to that particular conversation. This condition of trying to be accurate, objective, and complete, while realizing that there must be some interpretation or explanation that requires some subjectivity and which, in any case, is never complete, is not very different from the problems inherent in a journalist's report or the testimony of eye witnesses. In illustrating or analyzing interpersonal communication, you may wish to just give the facts of what transpired. The more you intentionally interject your own interpretations or preferences, the more you threaten the claim to reporting the truth. Between interpretive journalism or new journalism (à la Tom Wolfe) and fiction based on reality—such as Truman Capote's *In Cold Blood*—there are fewer distinctions than we might think. The one easily recognizable advantage of fiction is that the author disclaims a public responsibility to prove what he says. He or she cannot, I believe, be sued for libel, or have his or her report regarded as inferior because of deviations from objectivity. The fiction writer, unlike a journalist or social scientist, can claim to be an artist expressing a higher truth.

Students of interpersonal communication are, I think, more likely to value social science findings over artistic assertions and to want real examples rather than those chosen from fiction, poetry, drama, and other genres in literature. The problem is, however, that a good novelist is better at creating a sense of reality than are most social scientists or other reporters. Perhaps they are simply better writers. In any case, the analysis of interpersonal communication through fictional examples should not be dismissed because it is not true. Written truth is not true either, not, at least, if true means complete and understandable.

Erich Segal's *Love Story*, we are told, was based upon an actual incident. Even this may be fictional, of course, but that is not important. Segal is a good enough writer to create an illusion of reality. The novel's popular reception, which may have prompted suspicion among many critics, is an advantage for us. Because the novel is well-known, we need little background information. Moreover, because the novel is written from the first person or I-focused view, we have the illusion of entering into the conversation with the kind of subjective bias that is closest to our own conversations as we experience them. In addition, Segal, like any competent author writing in that point of view, gives us enough information to temper the subjective bias with a measure of critical objectivity. These are some of the qualities that literature provides that are usually not present in more factual reports of interpersonal communication, such as transcripts of tape-recorded conversations.

Moreover, as a work of fiction *Love Story* may be said to be unremarkable in nearly every respect except for its extraordinary popularity, not only in the United States but also abroad. Great literature, this is not. There are many clichés and few surprises. If the characters seem two-dimensional, that only makes it easier for the sort of simple application we seek here. Indeed, literature that is rich in overlayed symbolism and intricacies of style and innovation is probably not nearly as appropriate for this kind of application as is a slice-of-life daytime television series or Segal's *Love Story*.

In the fall of my senior year, I got into the habit of studying at the Radcliffe library. Not just to eye the cheese, although I admit that I liked to look. The place was quiet, nobody knew me, and the reserve books were less in demand. The day before one of my history hour exams, I still hadn't gotten around to reading the first book on the list, an endemic Harvard disease. I ambled over to the reserve desk to get one of the tomes that would bail me out on the morrow. There were two girls working there. One a tall tennis-anyone type, the other a bespectacled mouse type. I opted for Minnie Four-Eyes.

"Do you have *The Waning of the Middle Ages?*"

She shot a glance up at me.

"Do you have your own library?" she asked.

"Listen. Harvard is allowed to use the Radcliffe library."

"I'm not talking legality, Preppie, I'm talking ethics. You guys have five million books. We have a few lousy thousand."

Christ, a superior-being type! The kind who think since the ratio of Radcliffe to Harvard is five to one, the girls must be five times as smart. I normally cut these types to ribbons, but just then I badly needed that goddamn book.

"Listen, I need that goddamn book."

"Wouldja please watch your profanity, Preppie?"

"What makes you so sure I went to prep school?"

"You look stupid and rich," she said, removing her glasses.

"You're wrong," I protested. "I'm actually smart and poor."

"Oh, no, Preppie. I'm smart and poor."

She was staring straight at me. Her eyes were brown. Okay, maybe I look rich, but I wouldn't let some 'Cliffie—even one with pretty eyes—call me dumb.

"What the hell makes you so smart?" I asked.
"I wouldn't go for coffee with you," she answered.
"Listen—I wouldn't ask you."
"That," she replied, "is what makes you stupid."
Let me explain why I took her for coffee. . . .[1]

Love Story Analysis: Definitions of the Situation and Self-Image

How a person defines or perceives a certain situation will nearly always involve how the person perceives himself or herself. In the first passage quoted here, Oliver, who writes from the first person (I-focused) point of view gives us a fairly clear picture of his view of himself in this situation. The first sentence seems straightforward enough, but in the second sentence he uses a slang expression, "to eye the cheese," which puts him in the role of a mouse. A male chauvinist mouse, perhaps; it is a condescending attitude toward the Radcliffe girls. He continues with a more objective description of the situation as he sees it ("The place was quiet,") but then remarks "nobody knew me." The implication is that if he studied at Harvard so many people would talk to him or otherwise indicate recognition that he could not study well. Whether this is the case, we cannot know, but it may be that Oliver can heighten his sense of self-importance by going to the Radcliffe library as a place where nobody will bother him in order to tell himself ("If I were at Harvard, everybody would know me"). The next two sentences contain several pretentious, sophomoric (though he is a senior) expressions ("an endemic Harvard disease," "one of the tomes," and the mixed style "to bail me out on the morrow."). The reader may judge Oliver to be a jerk or just familiar college type, but the language suggests that Oliver thinks he is clever with the language and "in" with the college crowd. We then learn that he has a choice of approaching two girl library assistants, whom he describes in the same cavalier, gratuitous tone as before. In short, from his choice of language we can get some clue about Oliver's personality and self-image as well as his

[1] From pp. 2–3 in *Love Story* by Erich Segal. Copyright © 1970 by Erich Segal. Reprinted by permission of Harper & Row, Publishers, Inc. and Anthony Sheil Associates Limited.

view of the situation. This, of course, is part of the writer's craft, and this is fiction. But the same kind of interpretation could be made if there were a real Oliver telling us this.

In addition to what is stated or implied in the language, we also will supply our own assumptions about this kind of situation. What are the usual expectations, including appropriate role behaviors, of a person wanting to check out a book? Normally we might suppose a kind of complementary relationship; the borrower is in something of a guest or customer role, the librarian is in a kind of clerk role. He needs help, and her role is to supply the help. Their reasons for being there and their relationship to each other are not symmetrical, not the same at all. We should also expect a degree of role performance for the librarian—to be courteous, efficient, helpful, and businesslike.

Functionally, we should expect the main lines of conversation to be informative and instrumental. These descriptions, then, are also part of an expected definition of such a situation, though they are nowhere indicated in the dialogue.

The First Exchange

"Do you have *The Waning of the Middle Ages?*" The author gives us no clue as to how this was said, but lacking that information and given Oliver's point of view, we might assume it was said in a straightforward manner. The next line tells us that the girl's first response was nonverbal, hostile ("She *shot* a glance up at me.") followed by or synchronized with "Do you have your own library?" Two things are interesting here: (1) His question was met with another question—but not one to be answered as simply as Oliver's question might have been. It seems to be more of an assertion than a question and might be translated into: "You ought not to be here." His question seemed objective, hers somewhat personal and directed toward him. The "you" is also more ambiguous than it appears, because she does not know him personally (he probably assumes). "You" may refer to "you men" or "you Harvard men." Oliver seems to either interpret the meaning as the latter or to shift the argument to the latter personae. "Listen, Harvard is allowed to use the Radcliffe Library." Oliver now identifies with or represents Harvard, which he may feel strengthens his argument in a power play and which, incidentally, may further assert his own self-importance: "Me—Harvard: You—Mouse."

Thus far the language has been civil. This changes with the next remark, and the change may indicate a new phase of the encounter, the next step in the escalation. From Oliver's point of view, perhaps, he would punctuate the sequence to end it here. He ended her annoying questions by invoking a rule.

But the girl, Jennie, will not let it end. Instead she continues (or begins another round) by shifting from a technical rule to a philosophical claim: "I'm not talking legality, Preppie, I'm talking ethics." She continues, "You guys have five million books. We have a few lousy thousand." Several things are happening at once here, a great deal of information—particularly about their relationship—is being expressed. For one thing she has changed her style to a slangy, familiar style in the words "Preppie," "I'm talking ethics," and "a few lousy thousand." These are not the words of the efficient, courteous librarian. Moreover, she introduces the word that will carry the conversation for several more lines—"Preppie." This single word does two things at once: 1. It asserts that she knows something about him or about his type, and 2. she has an opinion—negative—about that.

It is difficult for any person to respond to all of that information immediately, not only in real life situations but even in literature where the carefully composed repartees are martialed more readily than is usually the case in life. The author inserts an indication of Oliver's feelings—largely annoyance with her and the dilemma of responding to her personally or acting otherwise in order to get the book.

It is at this point that the exchange might seem to be concluded from both persons' points of view. He returns to asking for the book as he did initially, though this time with more annoyance: "Listen, I need that goddamn book." The girl replies not to his expressed need but to his form of language. Moreover she half reverts to the librarian role. "Wouldja please watch your profanity, Preppie?" Again several things are happening in that single sentence. Author Segal's choice of "Wouldja" rather than "Would you" seems to emphasize a casual, cute style, not the language of a proper librarian; but the thrust of her request is very much in the librarian role. Please do not swear in the library. She also repeats the word "Preppie," either to try again what she tried before (including, perhaps, taunting previous Harvard men), or because she sensed that it was the word that provoked his swearing.

Oliver takes the bait—as he does throughout this book, playing straightman for Jenny—and in effect asks for clarification. "What makes you so sure I went to prep school?" This sentence, too, has several possible interpretations: 1. he is asking for information; 2. he is challenging her; 3. he may seem to be confirming her assertion by not denying it. And we should note again here that Oliver—any Oliver in such a situation—may not know exactly what he intends to express or to reveal.

This unit of exchange continues as Jenny replies to his question with a brief insult, "You look stupid and rich." And as she says this, she removes her glasses. As the reader comes to discover, the removal of the glasses is significant. But at the moment of removing them that act is open to several interpretations, including:

1. Even without my glasses you look stupid and rich.
2. I don't want to look at you anymore.
3. All the better to stare you down.
4. I have beautiful eyes—look at them and let that bother you even more.
5. I am flirting with you—let's see how you respond.

He tries to rebut, "You're wrong, I'm actually smart and poor." From his point of view, perhaps, he is stopping her retort by using her same pattern, but substituting the opposite adjectives. From her point of view, perhaps, she maintains control, having led him to imitate her style of speaking. In any case, she carries the pattern one more stage, using his whole sentence but using it to refer to herself. She also repeats the word "preppie," rubbing it in, teasing him.

The narration tells us that he is conscious not only of her eye behavior (her staring at him), but also of how pretty her eyes are. He seems momentarily torn between continuing the game and his attraction for her. The narration also makes clear that he views this girl both as a type—some 'Cliffie—and also as a particular individual (or at least a special case of the type)—a 'Cliffie with pretty eyes. Largely because of this confusion, he initiates the next round of sparring with a question that sounds like a perfect straight line. Literally and figuratively, he is asking for it!

Her reply is notable in several respects. First, it is unexpected; "I wouldn't go for coffee with you," is not the sort of response that he (or the reader) might have expected. Second, the reply shifts the emphasis from him or her to a comment about a future relationship involving both. Once again she has altered the level from surface content to relationship, though appearing to respond in terms of content. That is, her response is an answer to his question (content), but at the same time it raises new possibilities about their relationship. Third, because of the double thrust of this answer (content and relationship), it serves a double punctuation function. A question responded to by an answer should mark the end of an exchange. In this case it prompts another straight reply, which in turn allows the girl to add one more remark, which, in effect, completes that sequence. In other words, viewed from hindsight, her first response to his question was not the end of that sequence, as he might have thought, but was actually the initiation of or at least a continuation of her series of retorts, which concludes with: "That is what makes you stupid."

Although the girl's remark above seems to bring to an end the verbal interaction in the library (or what we are told of it in the novel), it only seems to set up Oliver so that he does invite her for coffee. The dialogue ended but not the dialectics of interaction, which we will treat in more detail in Chapter Seven.

From Oliver's point of view, the sequence progressed something like this:

1. A. I asked a question.
   B. She gave a sarcastic answer.
2. A. I told her the rules.
   B. She criticized me for being there.
3. A. I got angry and asked again for the book.
   B. She ignored my request and criticized me.
4. A. I challenged her criticism.
   B. She insulted me.
   C. So I insulted her.
   D. So she defended herself.

5. A. I asked her a sarcastic question.
   B. She gave a strange answer.
   C. I told her what I thought of her;
   D. She insulted me again.

From Jenny's point of view, the sequence might be segmented something like this:

1. This Harvard guy invaded our library.
   A. I told him to go to his own library.
   B. He said that "legally" he could use ours.
   C. So I told him that wasn't the point and implied he was not welcome.
2. A. He got angry and started swearing.
   B. So I told him not to swear and needled him about being a Preppie.
   C. This bugged him so he asked how I knew he went to prep school.
   D. So I told him he looked stupid and rich.
   E. He got defensive and said he was smart and poor.
   F. But I pointed out that I was the smart and poor one.
3. Actually he was kind of cute, so I thought I would tease him. I took off my glasses so he could see my beautiful eyes;
   A. He fell for me and asked me a dumb question.
   B. So I used the simplest kind of child psychology and set him up by saying I wouldn't want to have coffee with him.
   C. He said he wouldn't want to have coffee with me, either.
   D. So I insulted him again, which forced him to take me out for coffee.

Thus we have at least two points of view for segmenting and structuring this brief conversation, based on and also contributing to two different definitions of the situation. In a work of fiction of this kind, we may assume that these two points of view have been carefully crafted by the author in order to provide a basis for interpretation from yet another point of view—that of the reader. In this respect, then, fictional accounts may differ from real conversations. It may be, however, that when real a conversation between two persons takes place in the presence of third parties, the distinction between fiction and real life may be less relevant. Indeed, this is very close to the view of interpersonal communication as a kind of dramatic performance, a position taken by Erving Goffman, which we will discuss in Chapter Six.

FOUR
WE SPEAK
THE SAME LANGUAGE

The expression "the mother tongue," meaning one's native language, is more than trite poetry, for in a very real sense we are born into a particular language. Some might even say born from a language. A baby born in New York today will learn English or maybe Spanish and will very soon learn words that somebody else born in Bombay or Lagos will not learn. This is not simply a difference in sounds or grammar, but more importantly what the words represent and how words are used in communication with the baby's family and later in the larger society. What people talk about and how they talk about things is as much a part of language learning as is making the appropriate sounds and patterns of speech. During the earliest part of the child's life—from birth to about three or four years of age—the basics of the child's language are learned. It can be said that the mother tongue, as much as the mother herself, provides a sense of security, order, and consistency for the child. Learning the language, at least as much as learning other human behavior, such as walking on two feet, gives the child a sense of increasing freedom, even power over others. Indeed, before the child is aware of what is happening, the child finds that making certain sounds gives him a grasp of things even better than his clumsy hands might.

Infants exert no choice in the language they learn; they are totally dependent on others. A Vietnamese orphan plucked from his or her nation and reared by adopted parents in the United States will learn English, not Vietnamese, and that adopted mother tongue may exert as much influence on the child's later life as the adopted mother herself.

Perhaps nothing in interpersonal communication is more fundamental, more widely studied, yet more fragmented than the study of language. It is commonplace to say that the ability to use language is the crucial distinction between human beings and other animals. All animals and indeed even plants communicate, but only human beings employ a symbolic language that enables us to vicariously share in the experiences of others, including those who lived and wrote in the past, and to anticipate future courses of action. The ability to use language resides partly in the human brain, which has evolved to an extent that allows for such symbolic activity. In one sense, then, the ability to use language is biologically based and universal among human beings. But the kind of language we use and how it influences our communication is not a matter of biology nor is it universal.

Many communication scholars choose to ignore most of what is thought to be true of language and concentrate on the particular symbolic expressions that characterize a given human encounter. It may be wise, however, to view the phenomenon of language from several points of view before directing attention to examining any specific expressions in language in a given situation. At least three interrelated views of language should be recognized. One is that any language is systematic, conforming to implicit rules of pronounciation, grammar, vocabulary, and the like, which identify it as a particular language. Were it not reasonably systematic, a language could not be learned, let alone shared. The interest in language as a system has been the central interest of linguists, many of whom ignore all other aspects of language. But if language is a system, conforming to its own rules, it necessarily imposes restrictions and limitations. This seems true in two senses, as a medium and as a particular form of that medium. That is, while language, any language, allows extraordinary flexibility in what might be symbolized, language cannot quite be equivalent to what might be expressed in some other medium, such as a photograph, or a dance, or a physical embrace. Despite the capacity of spoken or written language, even when its resources are most fully used, it can only express what is expressible in language. Beyond this, each language has its own resources, its own genius some would say, which other languages or even other dialects of the same language do not. There are many words in English that cannot quite be expressed in other languages. There are slang expressions among in group members that have no exact equivalent in more orthodox expressions. As we will consider shortly, if we extend this thought far enough it suggests that any symbolic language may influence how we think we perceive, even what we think we perceive. Thus a second, disturbing, view of language is as a molder of our perceptions.

But how do we learn a language, and with whom do we speak the language? This question implies yet a third view of language that is crucial in studying interpersonal communication, that of language as an expression of identification with other persons.

These three views of language bear a strong resemblance to the three dimensions of semiotics, as proposed by language philosopher Charles Morris.[1] What Morris called syntactics, the relationship between symbol and symbol, views language as system; what he called semantics, the relationships between symbols and what they represent, is close to our idea of language as a molder of perceptions; and what he called pragmatics, the relationship between symbols and human behavior, covers in part our concern with language as identification. As we consider each of these areas briefly, keep in mind that all are interdependent. What we say must conform to rules, but in so conforming it may help to direct or shape the content of what is said; and anything that is said will be expressed to another who, to some extent, shares in those rules and that outlook.

Language As System

The number of possible sounds that a human being is capable of uttering is estimated to be in the thousands, and the combinations of those sounds beyond estimation. But a phonetician attempting to record the number of meaningful sounds within any language needs fewer than

[1] Charles Morris, *Signs, Language and Behavior.* (New York: Prentice-Hall, 1946).

fifty discrete markers, each of which may be modified somewhat. Spoken English, for example, uses only forty-five meaningful units— nine vowels, three semivowels, twenty-one consonants, four stresses, four pitches, and four junctures (meaningful pauses).[2] Indeed, the number of basic units in a language is small enough and systematic enough so that even an infant of only six weeks is already modifying his or her vocalizing in conformity with the system of the parents and others who surround the infant.[3] As a system, language—its sounds, its combinations into words and sentences, its inflections, and apparently the nonverbal expressiveness that accompanies speech—is relatively simple and consistent.

So language can be studied primarily as a system—of sounds, and sound combinations, and grammatical patterns, which are recognizable as part of a language—apart from what its expressions mean. Whether what is said seems true or false, profound or banal, is irrelevant if one is concerned primarily with the systematic patterns of the language itself. As an individual masters the possibilities of a language system, the person is able to express, not only what others say, but also what nobody else has ever said. That is, because we learn the patterns of a language and do not merely learn to repeat exactly what was said by others; everybody, including children—and perhaps especially children—can say things that have never been said before. What is more, others listening can usually understand what these totally new expressions might mean by, in effect, reversing the process.

Just as the number of possible sounds and combinations is greatly simplified in the system of any language, a language also serves to simplify the process of identifying and classifying the otherwise amorphous process of experienced reality. The number of people in the world, past and present, is very great indeed; the number of words we use, separately or in combination, to identify and classify those people is relatively small. Our experience of each day is somewhat different from all other days, but our systems for identifying a day by the calendar, or clock, or even by a variety of adjectives—hectic, short, un-

[2] Ray L. Birdwhistell, *Kinesics and Context*. (Philadelphia: University of Pennsylvania Press, 1970), p. 8.

[3] Some children do not express what is recognized as language until much later, including some famous cases of brilliant persons who did not utter a sentence until the age of four.

forgettable—permit, or require, these variable perceptions of reality to be stabilized and symbolized in a very limited way. Moreover, a language further reduces perceptions into even simpler, if broader, categories such as things, and events, and qualities. Rain, for example, may be treated as an event or more often as a collective thing, as in "The rain has stopped." Because English requires a subject and a predicate, comparable to some*thing* that *acts* in some way, we may say "it is raining," even though the "it" and the "is raining" seem to mean the same thing. In fact we must say something like that. We do not say "raining," for that does not sound like English; such an expression does not conform to the rules of the system of English. In other languages, however, comparable expressions are permissible within the systems of those languages. The point here is that when we share in and speak a language, any language, we are obliged to follow certain rules. From the perspective of some other language system such rules may seem quite arbitrary, but sounds, language categories, and grammar, are all arbitrary matters of convention and neither more nor less logical than the different possibilities found within the system of some other language.

Language as a system is arbitrary as a whole but obligatory for its speakers, simple and consistent in its structure but impressively flexible in its use. If we stop for a moment and speculate on the extensions of these brief observations, we may pass into another view of language that is much more controversial and, for many, far more fascinating in its implications. The language we speak may directly influence the reality we think we perceive, that language itself is a molder or shaper of perceptions and thought.

Language As Mold

Until this century it was generally assumed that thought was independent of language, that any language was merely a neutral medium through which thought could be codified and expressed. Then there appeared the speculations by Edward Sapir and Benjamin Lee Whorf, which argued that (1) because we appear to be compelled to think according to the categories and the logic of language, and because (2) languages differ in their categories and their implicit logics, thus (3) people who speak different languages will tend to perceive different realities according to the dictates of those languages.[4] To raise an earlier question, if a child grows up speaking Spanish and thus is required to distinguish between a familiar "you" (*tu*) and a formal "you" (*usted*), does he then also think of acquaintances differently from a child who speaks only English and has only one "you" in his language? Or what about a Japanese child who must in his language distinguish between older brother and younger brother because there is no single word equivalent to brother, for whom no plurals are used and whose grammar is markedly different from either English or Spanish? Are his perceptions different?

The basic question seems to be whether the particular language we speak influences the way we think and act. So far no way has been developed to answer that question, but it must be said that the evidence presented by Whorf and others propounding this theory has been seriously questioned. One criticism is the assumption that language can be isolated from other cultural forces in which the language is spoken. Language is a part of culture and of the implicit values, the social structure, and the physical characteristics of that culture. It is easy to find correlations between aspects of language and aspects of the culture in which it is spoken, but that does not prove that language influenced the culture; one might equally assert that the culture influenced the language. In the late 1960s or early 1970s, the word *Ms.* entered the American English vocabulary; but did the previous linguistic necessity of distinguishing between married and unmarried females (Miss or Mrs.) but not between married and unmarried males (Mr. for both) retard the movement for female equality with men? And will equality now be easier because of the word *Ms.?* It seems impossible to say one way or the other because words cannot be separated from their use.

Another criticism of the Whorfian arguments is that his translations of other languages, such as Hopi and Navaho, seem to be taken

---

[4] Similar speculations appeared much earlier—at least a half century before in the writings of von Humboldt. But Sapir really launched the broadest interest in the language-thought relationship, while his student Whorf carried the notion that our language strongly influences our perceptual and cognitive activities even further. For a wide-ranging debate on the issue, see Harry Hoijer, ed., *Language in Culture* (Chicago: University of Chicago Press, 1954).

too literally—that is, he compared a literal translation into English with a standard English equivalent and found some striking differences, which seemed to conform to other aspects of the respective cultures. But do we as English speakers respond to our own language literally? Do we have a feeling of being literally *in* something when we say: *"in* summer," *"in* the mood," *"in* trouble"? What of the Spanish speaker who, in literal translation into English, says "I am thinking in you" (*pienso en ti*), whereas we would say in English "I am thinking of (about) you." Are Spanish speakers' thoughts more intimate?

Yet another criticism of the Whorfian view is that it goes against the currently dominant theory of American linguists as advanced by Noam Chomsky in what is now called the standard theory.[5] According to this view, differences between languages are more apparent than real, more superficial than significant. Chomsky speaks of these as occurring on the "surface" of language, and he reasons that if one goes beneath the surface to a "deep structure" level, all languages will be found to be comparable. This school of thought, known as the generative transformational grammar school, emphasizes that language learning is one of the principles from which we generate new sentences, and that these principles are comparable from language to language. Thus a linguist can transform the surface form of a statement in one language into a comparable expression in any other language by going beneath the surface to the underlying principle.

However, we should be careful not to minimize surface expressions in the belief that at a deeper, theoretical level apparent differences can be equated. This may work for the transformational grammarian looking at language as a system unto itself and set to find universal linguistic principles, but it may not work for the people who are participating in communication. Assuming the language we speak and hear is expressed at a surface level, our immediate reactions, which influence our flow of communication, are likely to be no deeper. One does not have to penetrate very deeply to say that an expression like "ripping off Ma Bell" and "defrauding the American Telephone and Telegraph Company" really mean more or less the

---

[5] See Noam Chomsky, *Aspects of the Theory of Syntax* (Cambridge: MIT Press, 1965). For a less technical appraisal of Chomsky's theories and their significance, see John Lyons, *Chomsky* (London: William Collins and Co., 1970).

same thing. Still for some people, "ripping off Ma Bell" is a positive, political, philosophical, moral act committed against a symbol, at least, of a fat corporation. A lawyer for AT&T may not say it that way and may not see it that way.

Because we are not primarily interested in comparing possible influences on interpersonal communication or different languages, such as English or Spanish, we may do better to think in terms of language habits, which differ from person to person, from group to group, even though in a broader sense these people do seem to speak the same language.

It is tempting to try to resolve the dispute over the influence of language on perception, thought, and action by saying that the major participants in the controversy are viewing language in two different ways, or at two different levels. That is, as a biologically based system, language seems, from most of the evidence thus far, to be one of the human universals. In our usage of language, our language habits, however, we find greater diversity, and it is that concern with language that most interests us in the study of interpersonal communication.

Recent empirical evidence, which if further substantiated, may once more heat up the controversy over the influence of language. Until recently it has been taken as a universal principle of human behavior that the left hemisphere of the brain does the thinking (verbal analysis, mathematical calculation, and so on), while the right hemisphere serves our more emotive and aesthetic responses, such as the enjoyment of art or music. One phonologist, however, has found that for native Japanese speakers some stimuli that would normally activate the right hemisphere for speakers of other languages stimulates the left brain hemisphere for speakers of Japanese.[6] For most of us whose first language is not Japanese, the sound of a bird chirping, a baby crying, or a man snoring would seem to be responded to in the right hemisphere; for native Japanese speakers, such sounds are treated in the left side along with words. More recently, a group of UCLA scholars working with Hopi Indian children found that different parts of their brains were stimulated depending upon whether

[6] Tadanobu Tsunoda, "The Qualitative Differences in Cerebral Dominance for Vowel Sounds Between Japanese and European Languages," *Medicine and Biology*, Vol. 85 (Oct. 1972), pp. 157–162.

they were speaking English or Hopi—a finding that harks back to Whorf's first speculations. Such recent studies, of course, still do not prove that one's language shapes one's thinking, either at the fundamental level of brain responses or at the level of influencing human interaction. But they do serve to remind us of the profoundly complex influence of language on our behavior.

Language As Identification

Language in communication represents more than a human ability to share experiences and ideas through mutually intelligible noises. Language, any language, is in itself a symbol for identification. "We speak the same language," we may say, meaning we understand each other, and more, that we agree or share the same outlook. This is readily apparent across cultures. Churchill used to talk of "the English speaking peoples" of the world, and many Latin Americans feel a communality as much through their Spanish or Portuguese or French language as through geography and tradition. But the factor of language identification is equally apparent within a single nation, particularly in a country like the United States where different languages, different dialects, and a larger number of smaller groups can be found.

One of the clearest indications of language as identification is in the area of slang, the special in group language, which those who are "in" speak, half to show that they are "in," and half to help keep the others "out." Every college has some words or phrases or "in" jokes that are shared among its students, and probably an even larger number of expressions that reflect the separation of various groups on that campus. Some relate to special interests—the language of the surfers, the ski bums, the bikers, and those who major in theatre or in engineering. Blacks may have their own idiom, Chicanos theirs, Women's Libbers theirs. Over a period of time, distinctions among each of these will evolve to reflect the inevitable schisms that seem to develop in any special group.

Slang generally comes from below, from outside of the establishment and then into it—as with the enormous influence on American language from jazz, black slang, army slang, drug slang, gay slang, and so on. The effect is the co-opting of some of the language of the "outs" by the "ins." But apart from that, any group that feels a sense of "we" will develop, intentionally or not, a vocabulary and sometimes even a grammar, which both reflects and helps to direct its uniqueness. [7]

Some sociologists say that a generation, which used to be thought of as roughly twenty to twenty-five years (the parent-child difference in age), is now down to about four years or less on campuses, for the freshman and the senior don't speak exactly the same language. [8]

We participate in language. We do not invent a language, nobody does. We acquire our language without realizing it; we are born into a language. As we grow older and enter into new relationships, our language habits change. There are some striking differences between the language habits of a child at home and the habits of that same child after he has gone to school for a year or less, and most of these changes are not those taught in the classroom. This process continues through grade school, high school, and college; some language habits are discarded—often because they are associated with older attitudes, values, or experiences—and the new ones are learned. These habits may include new words, but also new rhythms and spacings of silences. Expressions may seem to have little content in themselves—"like, man, you know, man, like wow," but their content is identifiable with other expressions of an outlook on life. The use of what some English teachers would call vulgarities are typical—the so-called four letter words, which for some speakers seem to embellish every sentence—and serve important purposes, such as separation from straight speakers, informality and openness with another, liberation for some people, and so on. A person's language style will change according to the people with whom he or she is communicating. "Where it's at" is ungrammatical in a written theme for an English class. But with friends after class "where it's at" may be where it's at.

[7] Specialists, hobbyists, professionals, all develop such "in" language. Modern electronic and print media, which seem now to serve special interest groups better than the mass society, may increase this tendency even more than before.

[8] We are not being very precise about what is "a language," but language scholars are not too sure about a definition either. Norwegian and Swedish, for example, are no more different than what are called dialects in some other languages—but don't tell that to a Swede. And some linguists have argued that black English should really be regarded as a separate language since technically it differs sufficiently from standard American English to be treated as distinct.

The world is filled with countless things, events, and people; people are countable, perhaps, but if we add the awareness of change—that you are not the same person you were a month ago, biologically or otherwise—then we can say that there may be an infinite number of possible realities. But words are limited in number, as they must be if we are going to use language to think or to talk to one another. And so all of us who speak the same language will be using the same words to talk about quite different things. If we add to this observation the awareness that each person's self, experiences, background, outlook, and so on are also different, we can easily conclude that the same word probably never means exactly the same thing to any two people.[9]

Like-minded people often try to find new words for old realities in order to show that they have their own way of looking at reality. This, of course, is what most technical language is, and what a lot of slang is too. More pointedly, we can say that individuals may seek to create new realities by using new words or novel expressions. The word sounds themselves may seem familiar but their semantic meaning, what they represent, may be quite different; "a head," "a roach," "a freak," or "threads" probably evoke different reactions among people under thirty than for most people over forty. This principle allows some people to appear to be talking about one thing while actually talking about something else, a characteristic normally associated with poetry or humor, but not always so eloquent or funny. An early popular rock and roll song was "Dance with Me, Henry." The original version of the song was "Work with Me, Henry," a version that was played for a time on the radio until it became known that "work" meant "sex." "Work with Me, Henry" was banned; "Rock with Me, Henry," was born. Actually jazz slang (including the word *jazz*) is especially rich in double meanings and was allowed to enter the mainstream of American music and language largely because of such double meanings.

There are many misunderstandings that occur in conversations because two speakers use different words to refer to more or less the same thing, or use the same words to refer to quite different things.

---

[9] This familiar and terribly important principle is one of the simplest ways of distinguishing interpersonal communication from machine communication or abstracted studies like linguistics.

Probably no two people mean exactly the same thing when they use the same word, at least if we interpret meaning in the broad sense of experiences and associations with a particular word. If we would only assume that another person may have somewhat different reactions to a word, or may even have in mind some very different image, we could be more cautious in our conversations and perhaps avoid some of these simpler semantic problems. A related problem is assuming that there are right and wrong meanings for words, apart from the way a person uses them. Semantic correctness is simply a matter of agreement, either between the people speaking or more generally among most speakers of the language over a period of time. But apart from that there is no right or wrong.

Paralanguage

How something is said often determines what seems to be meant, for there are semantic and syntactic aspects of the ways in which the same words are spoken. Inflection, for example, nearly as much as word order, can determine whether the same words are meant as an assertion or a question. Take the words: "It's one o'clock." These might be said by a radio announcer giving the time. A person who hadn't realized how late it was might react with doubt, "It's one o'clock?" Another person might express shock or urgency, "It's one o'clock!" And we could add still other nuances to these same words (or almost any other words)—delight, secrecy, sadness, teasing, and so on. For some of these we would have to vary more than inflection; our loudness, pitch, voice tension, rate, rhythm, and pacing, all could vary. These are all qualities of speech that are sometimes identified as paralanguage, an aspect of communication to which most of us are likely to be much more sensitive than we might realize.

Children at a certain age are amused by paralanguage variations used in expressions to convey a double meaning, such as, "What are we having for breakfast, Mother?" Said one way, this is a question addressed to mother about breakfast. Said another way, the question seems to be about a breakfast that *is* mother. By making the slightest pause after the first sound in "ahead," we get a gruesome question that amuses children. "What's that in the road, ahead?" Even adults, sometimes by accident, seem to say one thing when they might have meant another. The sympathetic boss might say, "Miss Jones, my secretary, unfortunately is ill"; the critical boss might say, "Miss Jones, my secretary unfortunately, is ill." In such cases, inflection and pause (juncture) influence semantic meaning.

But the tone of voice or the elements of paralanguage mentioned previously are often more subtle and do far more than simply change the meaning of an utterance. If you have ever found yourself in a room with walls thin enough to allow you to overhear a muffled conversation in the next room, you know that even without clearly hearing the words that are said you can still guess from the tone of voice:

1. How many people are present.
2. Which sex or sexes they are.
3. The approximate ages of the people.
4. The mood of the conversation—angry, cheerful, serious, and so on.

Each person's voice quality is sufficiently different to allow special electronic devices to give a voice graph as unique as a person's fingerprints. And each of us is sufficiently sensitive to be able, usually, to recognize the voice of a friend who calls on the phone. But although the uniqueness of vocal quality and paralanguage is impressive, even more important in interpersonal communication is our ability to recognize from the tone of voice, even in strangers, moods of happiness, irony, eagerness, nervousness and so on. For we participate in these patterns, too; some are related to the physiological characteristics of a male or female, of a young person, or an older person. But most are learned and to a great extent controlled or monitored by us. This is most apparent in the voices of professional actors, actresses, and announcers who can turn on a voice that seems sexy or authoritative or concerned or whiney without much effort. And most of us are not so very different. A woman who makes her voice more breathy and uses some appropriate intonation patterns can sound sexier—like Marilyn Monroe's movie voice. By tensing the vocal cords most people will sound angrier.

Many years ago, Stan Freberg produced a phonograph record called "John and Marsha," in which a female and male radio performer carried on a complete dialogue just by using these two names in varying tones of voice to convey different feelings toward each other. More recently the French chanteuse Juliet Grecco sang a similar song using only one word in different tones of voice: *si*. [10] The great American actress of the turn of the century, Sara Bernhardt, was said to be able to bring an audience to tears by the way in which she could recite the alphabet.

Thus, simultaneously the paralinguistic aspects of speaking do several things: express something of the speaker's unique personality, indicate something of his or her mood at that moment, imply something about the speaker's relationship to the person he or she is talking with, sharpen the nuance of the sentence, and in some cases determine the meaning of the words expressed.

In interpersonal communication, these qualities of voice are not produced only with the diaphragm, larynx, mouth, tongue, and teeth in the way some textbook diagrams on speaking seem to show. Rather, it seems that the whole body—or even the whole setting and relationship to others present—helps to produce these qualities. Imagine for a moment that you are a military commander. Stand at attention, suck that stomach in, pull that chin in! Imagine the feeling of a tight fitting uniform with a stiff collar. Eyes forward! Now try barking out commands, "Tenshun!" And now, without changing your posture, try speaking in a casual style, "Hey, man, what's happenin'?" That uniform and posture, which are suited to that role in that situation, makes for a certain kind of crisp tone of voice that we associated with the military. To be sure there is a learned military style, which is also a part of the role performance, but the clothing and body position also contribute to that tone of voice.

Equally difficult is to try to make your voice sound as warm and friendly and smiley as possible, but without smiling. It is very hard to produce that very friendly tone of voice without actually twisting the face into a smile. And that is one reason we can see people talking on the phone, smiling, and nodding, and sometimes gesturing, even though the person at the other end cannot see this behavior. We have

[10] Perhaps *si* works even better than the John—and—Marsha pattern since even without paralinguistic variations *si* may mean "if" or "yes."

the impression that this might be even more true or more exaggerated in the case of long distance phone calls—as if we had to move the whole body to get our message across—or perhaps to get our money's worth. Another interpretation is that part of that smiling, nodding, bobbing, and the rest is behavior in reaction to what the other person is saying; it is a kind of listening behavior that influences our speaking behavior. And so here again we see why Birdwhistell says that "an individual does not communicate . . . he participates in communication," and why questions of structuring and punctuation are so very important in making any kind of realistic analysis of interpersonal communication.

But there is more evidence of a fascinating kind. An American psychologist, William Condon, has attempted to study interpersonal communication through the use of very slow motion films. By slowing down the film of a short segment of actual conversation and comparing the movements shown in the film with the words expressed by the people in the film, Condon has come up with a startling hypothesis. All of our body movements, even down to the smallest perceivable movements such as blinking an eye, appear to be synchronized to speech. When there is speaking no movement is free from speech; no movement is made at random. Rather it is as if speech were a kind of music and our movements, even our blinking, a kind of dance to that rhythm. According to Condon this holds true whether we are dancing to the music of our own speaking or to that of somebody else! Speaking is part of a total body process; or physical movement is a part of speech.[11]

Assuming that the rhythms of standard American English, and the rhythms of Spanish, or black English, or identifiable dialects of New York City English, or Tulsa, Oklahoma English and so on, are all somewhat different, we should not be surprised to find that the dances of the eyes, hands shoulders, and the whole body will also differ. Dance with me, Henry!

---

[11] William Condon and W. D. Ogston, "A Segmentation of Behavior," *Journal of Psychiatric Research*, Vol. 5 (1967), pp. 221–235; see also, John Condon and Fathi Yousef, *An Introduction to Intercultural Communication* (Indianapolis: Bobbs-Merrill, 1975), pp. 127–128.

The Digital and the Analogical

Two modes of expression serve to encompass much that we have looked at already and what we will look at in the next chapter. This is the distinction between analogical and digital forms of expression, a distinction originally based on two different kinds of computers and calculators.

The difference is fairly simple. In an analogical expression, both the content, or meaning, and the form are analogous; the shape or sound of the expression resembles what it stands for in some way. What we express and how we express it are analogous. In a digital expression, however, the relationship between the content and the form seems more arbitrarily assigned, must be learned, and cannot easily be guessed. Roman numerals seem more analogical than do most Arabic numbers. We can guess the meaning of the Roman II or the Chinese =, but the Arabic 2 doesn't look two-ish.

You may not know Chinese or Japanese, but you can probably guess the meanings of some characters. Japanese borrowed the Chinese characters that historically were based on pictures, or ideographs.[12] Even though you may not know Chinese or Japanese you might be able to correctly answer this analogical matching quiz. Try to match the ideographic characters (Japanese characters, originally from Chinese characters) with their meanings in English. (See bottom of page.)

If you did not know English, or Spanish, or any language written with a more or less phonetic alphabet, it would be difficult to guess what any one word represented from the word shapes. And similarly with speech—except for the language of onomatopoeia, words that are supposed to imitate sounds (ding dong, oink oink, and so on)—it is nearly impossible to guess the meaning of a word heard for the first time.[13]

---

[12] As spoken languages, Chinese and Japanese are totally different. Centuries ago the Japanese borrowed the Chinese writing system, much as English borrowed the Roman alphabet; by now, of course, there are also many differences between the written characters used for each language.

[13] Even in onomatopoeia, different languages express different sounds to imitate the apparently same noise. The sound of a dog barking is quite different in English, Greek, and Russian.

Answers: 1. b; 2. d; 3. c; 4. e; 5. f; 6. a.

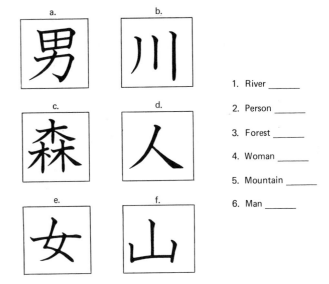

1. River _____

2. Person _____

3. Forest _____

4. Woman _____

5. Mountain _____

6. Man _____

You may already have anticipated the point of this discussion. The words of a spoken language are digital expressions. But to a great extent paralanguage—tones of voice, inflection, pitch, rate, and so on—is analogical. Usually, as excitement increases, our speech changes too—a greater rate, louder volume, and higher pitch. Try saying "I am exhausted" quickly and at a loud, high pitch (and without trying to sound funny).

Such discussion leads us to questions of relationships between words expressed and the way in which they are expressed and, as we shall see next, relationships between these two forms of expression and the kind of facial and body movement that is also expressive. But from what we have considered thus far we can imagine several possible relationships:

1. Parallel or harmonious expression of words and paralanguage. This, indeed, is what we might normally expect—sad words in a sad tone of voice and with a sad face, and so on. With this parallelism we can note the redundancy of expressing the same or similar content in different ways. Indeed this is so true of

We Speak the Same Language

most of our interpersonal communication that we need not perceive every sound and every subtle change in inflection in order to get the message another person may be trying to convey. As noted earlier, we are constantly filling in what we fail to perceive just as we are constantly failing to perceive every stimuli that presents itself.

2. Parallel or harmonious expression of words and paralanguage expression which, in particular combinations, reveal the uniqueness of the individual. Others can say the same words with more or less the same inflection, tone of voice, and so on, but not in exactly the same manner.

3. Parallel or harmonious expressions organized in such a way to emphasize the particular role or status (age, sex, and so on) of the speaker. Each of us is likely to change our tone of voice to fit the role we are cast in, or to emphasize our identification with a certain group at a certain time.

4. Varying the expressions in order to provide a particular nuance or attitude or mood, which is unique to that speaker at that moment. An expression of agreement like, "Yes, I agree . . ." can be said in a variety of ways that convey different degrees of agreement, from apparent certainty, to somewhat doubtful, to enough implied doubt as to mean, perhaps, "I don't agree."

5. Inconsistent or conflicting messages, where the words seem to say one thing but the tone of voice says the opposite. The previous example of agreement might be included here, but we so often hear this sort of expression that it may not strike us as particularly inconsistent. A more blatant example might be a he-man stock character (rugged look, tatoo,) speaking in a falsetto voice, or a person in an authority role who speaks with a quavering, soft voice. Such mixed expressions, of course, are often used for purposes of irony or humor.

As we will see in the next chapter, many of the same observations about paralinguistic aspects of our spoken communication also apply to expressions that are devoid of sound—our facial expressions, our gestures, our posture, and even our clothing.

The Meanings of Verbal Meaning

There are thousands of books about language, but very few say much about interpersonal communication. Those who have studied language often believe, wisely or blindly, that to step outside of language as a system unto itself is to step into the quicksand of personal differences that prevent further advances in linguistic science. Many regard the question of meaning in much the same way. Yet in a study of interpersonal communication we may also feel frustrated with theories and findings about language as a system that reveal little about people participating in communication. We must be concerned with meaning, not merely of word meanings, but meaning in a much broader sense; our entire study is about meaning. Semiotics, which we mentioned previously, provides some rough distinctions for separating our interest in meaning in language and other symbolic forms from other aspects of language. Most studies of language have concentrated on the syntactic dimension, but our interest is much more pragmatic. Let us briefly review these three semiotic themes with respect to the meaning of meaning.

In a linguistic tradition, meaning at one level is any difference that makes a difference. A celebrated linguist like Kenneth Pike in one of his famous monolingual demonstrations can interact with a person he has never met, who speaks in a language he has never heard before and has no knowledge of, and within an hour usually identify all of the meaningful sounds (phonemes) within that language, describe some aspects of the grammar, and probably identify and appropriate equivalents in English for several of the words. This is the method that many linguists or anthropologists use when going into a new culture to learn a language from scratch. What happens in these exchanges is that the linguist discovers which of the sounds (and later larger units, such as grammar) seem to make a difference.

While coming from a very different perspective, Kenneth Boulding has proposed a similar criterion for meaning when he writes about people's images: "information" or "meaningful communication" is anything that makes a difference in one's image of himself, society, and the world.[14]

[14] Kenneth Boulding, *The Image* (Ann Arbor: Ann Arbor Paperbacks, 1961).

Between these two extremes—differences in sounds and differences in images—lies an important part of meaning. Thus part of the meaning of a dress, let us say, may be whether the length of the hemline makes a difference or the color makes a difference. The differences may be situational (black or dark blue may make no difference in a party dress, apart from one's preference; at a funeral it may make a difference and hence, color becomes meaningful, or is part of what is communicated by the color of the dress).

Another criterion for meaning, not unrelated to the previous standard, is the way in which something—a word, a facial expression, hairstyle—fits into a shared code. As we shall see later, this is similar to the distinction between information and noise in the cybernetic model of communication. At the level of sound alone, "bit," "but," and "bot" are all perceived as different in English, and hence the *i*, *e*, and *o* sounds are meaningful. At the level of words, however, only the first two seem meaningful; there is no entry for "bot" in the dictionary. In conversation you can say "but I don't know," or "bot I don't know," and the meaning is the same. Or consider the ubiquitous word "uh." There may be times when the "uh" seems to mean that the speaker is unsure of himself or hesitant about something, but if you listen closely to almost any conversation in English you will find a surprisingly large number of "uhs" in our speaking, which do not seem to mean much of anything at all. And when we listen to somebody speaking, unless there seem to be too many "uhs," we are likely to ignore them. They are not functional. They are never punched onto computer cards or included in telegrams. If a foreigner tries to learn English through hearing a native speaker, he may at first not know if the "uh" is meaningful or not. He might even try to look the word up in the dictionary because it is quite possible there is no such sound in his own language. So to this extent the second criterion is somewhat different from the first.

One problem with this approach is that some expressions—verbal or otherwise—may be part of some people's code or of one individual's code, but not of a widely shared code. And it may be something that the individual is not fully conscious of. A psychiatrist, for example, may notice that one of his patients always arrives about ten minutes late for an appointment. Another patient always comes early. If this happens often enough, the psychiatrist may interpret the time of arrival as meaningful, which is to say an unspoken commentary about the sessions. Neither of the patients may be consciously aware of this, and indeed, as suggested earlier in the book, this pattern may be the result of the psychiatrist's own projection. This, of course, is the basis for many stock jokes about psychiatrists—that they are always finding hidden meanings when none exists. Recall the story of two psychiatrists passing on the street: one says, "hello," and the other thinks, "I wonder what he meant by that?"

What we usually think of as language is the fullest, most explicit, symbolic coding of referents, experiences, events, and so on. But, as we have said, it is only one of many such codes. To a considerable extent the contemporary study of interpersonal communication is an attempt to discover patterns of behavior or codes that we had not previously been aware of. One of the clearest recent examples is Edward Hall's pioneering research into *proxemics*, the study of the "meaning of interpersonal distance," which we will discuss in Chapter Five.

A third and much broader criterion for meaning, similar to that emphasized by the general semantics school of Alfred Korzybski, views meaning as virtually any biological or physiological reaction to a signal, or symbol, or symbolic act.[15] Ultimately, I suppose, to know the meaning of anything for any one person, you would have to do something to see how the person reacts internally. But at a more overt level, you would simply see how people respond externally to any symbolic stimulus. Meaning, in short, is not contained in the word or stimulus as it differs from similar ones, nor in its capability of fitting within some pattern or code, but in the reaction it produces in any one person.

An example may help to clarify this distinction. The word *rape* is recognizable as a word in English. It uses sounds (and, as printed, letters) that are part of the expressive coding system known as the English language. In different contexts it has different meanings. There is, for example, a flower called rape. In the Richard Lester film *The Knack* or in Voltaire's *Candide*, rape is a subject of laughter, though the normal reaction is anything but funny. Thus one cannot explain the

[15] Alfred Korzybski, *Science and Sanity; An Introduction to Non-Aristotelian Systems and General Semantics* (Lancaster, Penn.: Science Press, 1933). For a briefer account see also, John Condon, *Semantics and Communication*, 2nd ed. (New York: Macmillan, 1975).

meaning of rape apart from the context. Some people may experience an almost perceptible physiological reaction when hearing the word or even reading the word *rape*. For our third criterion, then, the meaning of rape must certainly include that reaction, however similar or dissimilar it may be to other reactions. I mention this example primarily because of some widely publicized advice offered to women by the New York City Police Department. Among many suggestions for self-protection, the police added this: *"If you are attacked, scream 'fire.' It will bring people to help you faster than yelling 'rape.' "* It is that sort of meaning, not given by a dictionary, which most concerns our study of interpersonal communication. It is a meaning that arises out of experiences as revealed in human reactions.

A number of techniques have been used in recent years to make some of these subjective reactions more objective, to render the privacy of meaning public. Some techniques are cumbersome, such as galvanic skin response tests or the use of the lie detector machine. Others require the analysis of recorded voice transcripts to determine tenseness and to infer certain qualities, such as honesty. Such methods recently received wide publicity with the analysis of President Nixon's White House tapes and Patty Hearst's taped messages as an S.L.A. captive and member. The semantic differential developed by Charles Osgood is more widely used by communication researchers. This method simply presents a printed form with the word, expression, or phrase whose meaning is to be interpreted along with a series of polar terms, such as good-bad, strong-weak, cold-hot, and so on. Persons indicate where in the range of responses for each of these scales he or she would score the word being studied, and simple statistical formulae then plot the meaning of the word in terms of those dimensions. Using the semantic differential method, reactions to similar words, such as *fat* and *overweight* can be compared, changes in meaning over a period of time can be noted, and different individual reactions can be compared. But there are some obvious disadvantages in such methods, including the isolation of a word or phrase from its verbal and social context, the time required, and the determination of meaning within the terms of the particular research system rather than the interpersonal system of the moment.

The meaning of verbal meaning thus ranges from perception of some stimulus as fitting into an established code, all the way to the reactions, subtle or gross, of the person expressing or perceiving that stimulus. The stimulus may be a word, a glance, a shoe dangling from a toe, or a flag. But in human communication, interpersonal communication, it is not likely to be any single stimulus, but rather the entire constellation of stimuli as perceived by any one individual, which are filtered and shaped by the countless past experiences of the individual. One cannot meaningfully talk about the meaning of a word, or smile, or an action individually, nor can one really talk about the meaning of anything; each person is likely to respond in a somewhat different manner.

But where does that leave us? If all meaning were entirely personal, there could scarcely be communication. But if meaning were entirely public, or like one computer processing the data from another computer, there might not be so much to communicate about. So it seems that for human communication or interpersonal communication, the meaning of meaning is a bit of both, the precise mixture depending on the person, the situation, and the topic. The poet does his or her best to express in the public symbols—words—the poet's personal meaning or inspiration. The antonym of poetry is cliché, the possibly unique inspiration rendered into its most public, most predictable, form. The dullest people (and sometimes the most reassuring) are the most predictable.

Here there is an irony in the study of interpersonal communication. If we had the formulae and the methodology to identify and make meaning objective for analysis, then we could carry our study to its conclusion. Eager students of communication seem to have such an end in mind—the ultimate theory or method that would encompass everything. Surely only the most reactionary could be unhappy at such a prospect. Only one who would want to leave room for chance, or uniqueness, or intuition, or whatever term describes that which would elude analysis. But, in fact, there are probably no scholars who entertain a hope of eventually being able to explain everything. "If they give you ruled paper," Juan Carlos Jiménez wrote, "write the other way." In American slang, if "bad" means something negative, then let the "baddest mother" be the best. If college means success, financial achievement, praise, then drop out and do better. Verbal meaning, sometimes, would rather reverse itself or destroy itself, than be made public. Verbal meaning, as with almost any other term in the study of interpersonal communication, ultimately eludes the grasp of the explainers.

Perhaps we must revise some of our basic notions of meaning if we are to use that word in an understanding of interpersonal communication. We might begin by recognizing that meaning can be—or perhaps must be—interpreted at different levels. That is, an hour's monologue may be regarded as having essentially a single meaning, but also each segment (down to each pause or inflection) may have other meanings. Perhaps we should think more in terms of meanings in the plural rather than *the meaning* if we recognize that each participant in the communication will have somewhat different responses and that each view, in its own way, is as valid and relevant as any other. This would imply that we also abandon any notion that the primary meaning of any word or action is to be determined by the one who expresses the word or action. Similarly, yet this may seem more radical, perhaps we should not assume that the outside observer or analyst is in the best position to determine the real meanings of what transpires in interpersonal communication. Our interpretations may be different, but they are not necessarily any more real by being more detached. They may be more precise or more suited for analysis, comparison, even prediction—goals expressed by some who study interpersonal communication as a science—but that is something else. Rather, the point is simply the perception of an abstract concept like *meaning* is relative, depending upon the perspective, set, or definition of the situation. In this sense it is like the perception of anything else.

Summary

Any interpretation of language in interpersonal communication is concerned with meaning, and yet the full meaning of any communication act goes beyond what is expressed in language. Words expressed may be the most public and accessible form of communication to be shared and to some extent to be understood. And yet the meaning of the words spoken by any person to any other must always lie at least partially beyond the interpretation of any observer. We would do well to recognize at least three qualities of any verbal expression and to appreciate how these three are related. Whatever is said will conform, to a great extent, to the requirements and patterns of the language in which it is expressed. To be meaningful, an expression must therefore conform to patterns shared by countless others who speak the same language. But also what is said will be influenced by and given shape by that language system. We talk about what our language allows us to talk about, and we express our ideas only within the categories provided for us. Perhaps everybody talks about the weather, but *how* each person talks will be determined to a great extent by the vocabulary available; the urban meteorologist, the Kansas farmer, and the airline pilot may all talk about the weather in very different ways. In part even the kind of weather they perceive is different, but also their language resources for talking are different. Equally important, what any one person says—about the weather or anything else—is in turn influenced by who the person is talking to. Both intentionally and without much conscious thought we alter our style of speaking and the words we use depending on the situation and the particular person or persons with whom we speak.

We can easily recall a conversation where we listened to a person who spoke our language, who used a variety of relatively precise and objective sounding words but who, in some sense, did not communicate, or who did communicate an impression of pomposity or peevishness more than content. We can also recall very meaningful conversations in which the number and variety of words exchanged was rather small; in a sense not much was said, but much was communicated. In such contrasting situations language for alienation or identification may be more crucial than the grammatical patterns or semantic categories expressed.

We have discussed language apart from facial expressions, gestures, and the settings in which people use the language, but this is an artificial distinction. Until fairly recently, the interest in communication was almost entirely in verbal communication; today we recognize that nonverbal expressiveness should not be ignored or even treated separately from verbal behavior. As a matter of convenience in this book, the discussion of the verbal and nonverbal is divided into two chapters, but in reality there is no neat distinction. We should also note that much that we have considered about language in this chapter will also apply and guide us in the following chapter on other forms of symbolic expressiveness.

FIVE
NOT IN
SO MANY WORDS

The great musical event in the United States in 1968 was the opening of the tribal rock musical, "Hair." To the older generation it must have seemed an unlikely title for a musical, but for millions of youth no greater rallying symbol of the era could be found than hair. So much meaning was compressed into that symbol, as the title song said, "Gimme hair . . . Hair, I adore it, gimme hair like Jesus wore it, Jesus' mother loved her son, why don't you love me, Mother, hair, hair, *hair*. [1]

From roughly the time of the emergence of the Beatles in the United States, long hair became a symbol of identification among youth who dug the same kind of music, the same kind of political outlook, the same expanded religious outlook, and the same life-style. "Hair" was about all of these. In time, of course, long hair, like any other fashion, spread even to the straight establishment. But for years, hair was a symbol of identification among some and defiant separation for others. Many a high school student fought the administration for the right to wear his hair like he wanted to wear it and not like the

[1] "Hair," from the musical of the same name; lyrics by Gerome Ragni and James Rado; music by Galt MacDermot.

principal or board of education wanted it. My hair, right or wrong. Cases went as far as the Supreme Court.

Among the Black community afros were hair symbols of black pride, black power, a visible sign for brothers and sisters.[2] Joan Baez's hair style, as much as her singing style, became a model for a generation of young women. Beards came in, and in the permissive society even pubic hair became public hair.

Considering all of the possible ways in which the human body participates in communication—posture, hand gestures, facial expressions, eye contact, and much more that we will want to look at—hair might seem relatively unimportant. But important or not, it serves as a model for questions about nonverbal communication and how it might best be studied.

One possibility arises from centuries of symbols of hair—or hands or eyes—and the feeling that there might be something very basic, even primitve, in our response to nonverbal expressions. We think of the symbolism of Samson's hair, of god images with long hair and beards, of the themes in Western literature in which men seemed to have loved becoming entangled in the hair of women, of the locks of hair kept in, naturally, lockets. George B. Leonard and Marshall McLuhan in their essay "The Future of Sex" have commented on the meaning of the hair styles of the Beatles and their early imitators: [3]

> What are those young men with long, flowing hair really saying? In what may seem to be a ludicrous overstatement, they are sending a clear message to all who will listen: 'We are no longer afraid to display what *you* may call 'feminine.' We are willing to reveal that we have feelings, weaknesses, tenderness—that we are human. And, by the way, we just may be ridiculing all of those up-tight movie males with cropped hair and unflinching eyes. We're betting they can't touch our girls.' Indeed, the long-haired boys' appeal is not esthetic, but sexual; not private, but corporate.

The previous quotation seems especially significant not only for the case of the long hair but for much of nonverbal symbolism.

---

[2] The afro was a uniquely North American hair style; several African nations prohibited it in their countries for several years.

[3] George B. Leonard and Marshall McLuhan, "The Future of Sex" in *The Man and Woman Thing and Other Provocations*, ed. George B. Leonard (New York: Dell Publishing Co., 1970), p. 146.

Clearly, the public reaction was to something more deep-rooted than aesthetics or preferences of style. The very intensity of the reaction suggested that the straight people were getting a message of something as fundamental as sexuality; a society does not become so upset over matters of preference but it does when the issue is one of values. Moreover, as Leonard and McLuhan say, the appeal was corporate, not private—much like other social movements before or after (black power, women's liberation, antiwar movements, and the like).

These observations, in turn, relate to our previous consideration of language and mark a departure that is significant for nonverbal symbolism. First is the expression of identification (corporate, not private). The uptight matron who was first startled by the long hair could "see one and she'd seen them all." But at the same time, a nonverbal expression of this kind cannot be debated or challenged on its own terms; one can't fight hair with hair. Express an idea in words and another can dispute, can show contradictions or limitations; nonverbal expressions may be approved or disapproved but they are not debatable nonverbally. So one approach to the nonverbal expressions in communication might be in the tradition of the humanities or even in anthropology, in which scholars have sought to discover the archetypal symbols to which humanity has responded throughout time.

The Nonverbal As Analogical

Consistent with this approach is to consider most nonverbal expressions as primarily analogical, in the distinction made previously in connection with paralanguage. To symbolize the loss of individuality and the subjection to the will of the group, hair is shorn in the military, in the convent, or in prison. The public speaker who verbally embraces "all of you wonderful people" may, analogically, open his arms as if to physically embrace them. The fearful, defensive person postures his body in a closed, protective manner—shoulders hunched together, arms across his chest, head tucked down, eyes narrowed. Much of the popular writing and training in nonverbal communication has emphasized this approach—the body as the analogue of the state of mind.[4]

---

[4] By now there are many books on the subject. One of the more complete, with respect to theory and experience, is William Schutz, Joy (New York: Grove Press, 1967).

A Swiss psychologist, Robert U. Akeret, has produced an intriguing book called *Photoanalysis: How to Interpret the Hidden Meanings of Public and Private Photographs*, in which this analogical approach is used throughout; but where analysis ends and projection begins is sometimes hard to tell. Akeret includes in his book a baby picture of former President Nixon at age nine months and a photograph taken in 1972. The psychologist split the photographs vertically down the center to divide the face in half, revealing a kind of "giocanda smile" (like that of the Mona Lisa). He comments:

> The left side of his face shows a beginning to smirk, the verge of a smile. But the right side is controlled and depressed, full of sadness. Look back at the baby picture. His right side is the one that shows the restraint, and although unsuccessful, it is his left side that attempts some form of social communication through the wave of the left hand.

> Having looked at dozens of photos of Richard Nixon, I am struck by the same incongruence of left and right sides. But why? Why are there two separate faces of Richard Nixon, both expressed at the same time? We cannot state categorical conclusions just on the basis of photographs. But we can ask some probing questions.

> Is it that his inner emotions are split down the middle, in conflict, with neither side of his personality ever winning out? [5]

In so-called sensitivity training programs the theme of the body as an analogue of the mind is stressed. One writer has urged people who are having verbal fights to change to nonverbal, physical fights; only then are the feelings truly expressed. [6] (A marriage counselor has also suggested that husband and wife should physically fight out some marital problems—leading to the quip that the marriage vow should be changed from "with this ring I thee wed" to "*in* this ring I thee wed.") Sensitivity training exercises have included trust circles, in which one person is blindfolded, placed in the center of a group, and urged to walk freely across the circle until reaching the people on the other side

[5] Robert U. Akeret, *Photoanalysis; How to Interpret the Hidden Psychological Meaning of Personal and Public Photographs*, ed. Thomas Humber (New York: Peter H. Wyden, Inc., 1973), p. 132.

[6] Schutz, *Joy*, pp. 156–169.

who then turn and guide the person back into the circle. The distrustful person exposes his or her state of mind by timid, fearful steps, as if something dreadful would happen; as trust develops, the person walks freely, knowing that he or she will be protected and guided. And following the exercise, it is hoped that this sense of interpersonal trust remains. The body tutors the mind.

A similar exercise is used in some kindergarten programs, particularly in the Montessori schools. An oval ring is painted on the floor of the classroom, and children practice walking on the line around the ring. Children who are emotionally upset, whose thoughts are scattered, or who seem flighty cannot walk smoothly without stepping outside or inside or losing their balance. Happy, emotionally stable children can. More importantly, it is said that through the walking exercise the nervous or distracted child learns to coordinate mind and body and becomes calmer, better adjusted.

There are, by now, dozens of books of related exercises that emphasize the analogical aspects of body and mind, the altering of personalitites and improvement of interpersonal communication through nonverbal relating. Bound up with the analogical assumtion is usually another assumption—that our body movements, from gestures to facial expressions to walking, are far less under our conscious control than is our speaking behavior. Our words may lie but our bodies cannot—or at least not as easily. And it follows from this assumption that if there is an inconsistency between what one's words seem to say and what one's body seems to say, we are likely to believe in the body expressions rather than the words.

And the Digital

We cannot go very far in this discussion without coming up against one of the basic controversies in nearly any study of human behavior—nature vs. nurture, or the difficulty of separating what is natural, or innate, or universally characteristic of human beings from what is nurtured, taught and learned, and thus characteristic of a specific group, such as a culture. The analogical theme, of course, leans toward nature. The digital theme is clearly in the camp of nurture. The stakes are high in this sort of dispute. If most of our nonverbal expressions are analogical, then we will have a much easier time of recognizing what is communicated; the body speaks a universal language. But if most of our behavior is learned, like our language, then it may take many years of systematic study to crack the codes of the nonverbal languages.

Ray L. Birdwhistell, whose name has come up often, has urged us to look at nonverbal communication as if it were a language, and he has used the term that is now current for the study of meaningful nonverbal expressions, *kinesics*, as a counterpart to *linguistics*, the study of spoken language. He has worked to develop a specialized vocabulary and shorthand system for coding nonverbal expressiveness. Certainly this is necessary if we are to be precise about what it is we think we are reacting to, for our ordinary language about bodily expressions is notoriously vague. (What is a smile, or a frown, or a look of puzzlement? Indeed, what parts of the face and body express those reactions?) Birdwhistell's attempts are impressive. But also formidable and difficult. And, alas, maybe not complete or precise enough.

To take a simple and often quoted example, Birdwhistell reports that a motion picture camera can record up to 1,000 positions of the eyelid, from wide open to tightly shut. But people are not cameras; people seem to be able to identify only eleven of those possible positions. And, he says, of these eleven, only four are meaningful, at least for North Americans.[7] How to identify those four in words and coding notions for analysis is the next stage. Because eyelids do not open and close in isolation, we must also try to recognize all of the other movements of the face—the brow, the mouth, chin, and so on—and the posture and gestures that accompany the eye openings in some patterns. And beyond this we must take account of the situation—who, where, when, and so on. Complicated and fascinating.

If we wish to better understand interpersonal communication as it occurs, particularly when we are a part of it, we want something simpler than kinesic analysis, but more complex than simplistic analogical notions.

We might start with a few guidelines.

---

[7] Ray L. Birdwhistell, "Kinesics and Communication," in *Explorations in Communications*, eds. *Edmund Carpenter and Marshall McLuhan* (Boston: Beacon Press, 1960), 54–64.

1. Many nonverbal expressions are used as substitutes for words. These we can assume are, like speech, digital, learned, have different meanings in different contexts, and are subject to misunderstanding. The thumb and forefinger symbolize okay in much of the world; it also means money among the Japanese, and when modified by using the index finger it is, in parts of Northern Africa, a prostitute's solicitation. Though there is something analogical about all three of these meanings, the exact usage must be learned—just like the meaning of okay, which is by now one of the most universally spoken words borrowed from English.

Special groups often develop sign codes; most grade school children do so as part of their language of clique identification, and secret or illegal societies do the same for related reasons. The sign language of the deaf probably also serves some purpose of group identification, but they clearly use sign language as a practical substitute for the words that they cannot hear. At the stock exchange or in almost any trading activity where large crowds prevent easy vocal exchange, hand language (sign language) is used. And this must be learned. Even more familiar is the football referee whose whole body is used to signal touchdown, holding penalty, and so on, a specialized language recognized by millions of football fans.

The gesture language of the stock broker or the football referee serves not only as a substitute for speaking when distance or crowding makes speech impossible, but also constitutes a part of role behaviors. Thus many of these gestures are performed in a manner that enhances the authority role of the user. Many forms of sign language serve the dual purpose of signaling and expressing role behavior to two different audiences. An orchestra leader, for example, communicates with the audience at his rear as well as with the orchestra.

2. Another function of gestures and other bodily movements is that of amplifying or qualifying what one is saying. As we saw in the last chapter, when we express ourselves in words, our whole body (and that of our listeners) reacts in synchrony. Our nodding, shifting, hand movement, and even our blinking seem to be inevitably synchronized to the rhythms of our speech. But at the same time, our bodies will respond as our paralanguage, giving special emphasis or qualification to what we are saying. Turn down the volume of a TV set and watch the movements of the speakers; you can often guess fairly accurately

that this part of a speech is important, or that part is a matter of speculation, merely by watching the speaker's body. His shoulders shrug slightly, he turns his head slightly and glances upward, pausing—his body seems to say; "well . . . maybe . . . I'm not sure . . ." Most of these bodily expressions are not performed consciously, except in special cases of professional actors or some public speakers, who may have rehearsed their movements as well as their words. These movements, then, do not substitute for words, but accompany them and qualify and clarify what is said. So these seem more on the analogical side.

3. The previous examples seem to give emphasis to the person who is speaking. If we wish to add a separate category for a person who is primarily a listener during some segment of communication, we could note the listening function of basically the same sort of gestures. Ekman and Friesen,[8] two of the leading researchers in this field at present, have proposed a separate category for these *regulators*— expressions serving to inform the speaker that he is being understood or not understood, going too quickly or too slowly, and so on. Here, too, we could include the speaker's own gestures to indicate that he expects the other person to speak or acknowledge his understanding.

4. Many of our gestures reflect our internal feelings quite apart from an interpersonal communication situation. Maurice Kraut has labeled these *autistic gestures*, and Kraut, a psychologist, used to observe such expressions performed by his patients while they were still in the waiting room.[9] Kraut felt, as others including Freud have felt, that these expressions often provide more and better insights into a person than the gestures or words expressed in front of others. Nervous gestures—rubbing hands together, picking lint or dandruff from one's clothes, the woman subtly covering the collar of her blouse with her hand, or men hitching their pants—are familiar examples. Certainly it is possible to intentionally affect autistic gestures to convey a feeling of nervousness or embarrassment, even when one does not actually feel that way. In Japan, girls and women cover their mouths with their

[8] Paul Ekman and Wallace Friesen, "The Repetoire of Nonverbal Behavior: Categories, Origins, Usage, and Coding," *Semiotics*, Vol. 1 (1969), pp. 63–92.

[9] Maurice Kraut, "Symbolic Gestures in the Clinical Study of Personality," *Transactions of the Illinois State Academy of Science*, 24 (1931), pp. 519–523.

hands to express embarrassment, but this is less often an unconscious gesture as it is a conscious expression of femininity—to be feminine in Japan is to be a little embarrassed.

5. If interpersonal communication includes all of our behavior, then most of our behavior will be nonverbal and most of this probably lies outside the four categories mentioned previously. Enter a waiting room at a bus terminal or airport, and the communication you observe is that of people waiting. This includes how people sit or stand or where they are standing—in a line, at a ticket counter, by a phone booth, and so on. Their very presence in a particular position at a particular location communicates.

Although this seems so obvious as to be not worth mentioning, in recent years scholars have come to recognize that even this seemingly natural behavior is, in fact, largely learned behavior. One of the clearest examples of this, which also cuts across several of the previous functions, is that of the distance between people when they communicate. Physical distances between people vary from culture to culture, and within a single society different distances correspond to other more apparent aspects of interpersonal communication. This special area is known as *proxemics*, a term and subject introduced by anthropologist Edward Hall.[10] How far apart do two people stand when they are engaged in a casual conversation? What if they are good friends or strangers, both men or both women, or a man and a woman? What happens when one comes too close or moves too far away? What is too close? What is too far? Too close or too far for what—saying hello or telling a secret? What if there are chairs and a sofa, or a table with chairs? There are many such factors and by now enough studies to give some detailed answers to at least some of these questions for some cultures. This is not the book in which to go into details (see bibliography for some recommended works), but we mention this to make the point that interpersonal distance seems to conform to some rules that we learn without realizing it—until things are wrong and somebody is too close or too far away. Perhaps because proxemic behavior is easier to observe and describe than subtler expressions—such as facial expressions—it has come to provide one of the most frequently cited proofs that most of our seemingly natural behavior is actually learned. And

[10] Edward T. Hall, *The Hidden Dimension* (New York: Doubleday, 1966).

like our language, it appears that we can learn to read the language of the body with accuracy.

But here comes the catch. Popular books that purport to tell how you can learn to read the language of the body sometimes get caught in a digital-analogical, nature-nurture trap. The most appealing examples of body language tend to be of an analogical, natural kind— the man with his arms folded across his chest is defensive, is protecting his mental set just as his arms protect his body. But the examples that lend authority through careful studies by "the experts" tend to be of a digital kind—the sort that may take hundreds of hours of analysis before the results are in. This is hardly speed reading of the body. To complicate things further, a common theme in such writings is that the body language cannot tell lies the way our spoken language can, and hence if one learns to read the secret language of the body, one can penetrate another's inner moods and thoughts. But if this is so, what then of the person who has read such a book and does indeed alter his or her behavior to create an impression of naturalness? The problem seems to be not so much in the inconsistencies of the popular treatments of body language, but in the likelihood that there is some truth in each of these points of view. If we are at all serious about understanding our nonverbal expressiveness in interpersonal communication, we must be somewhat cautious. There is a great difference between reading and reading *into* the expressions of others.

If nonverbal expressiveness can be likened to a language, it is interesting that most efforts, with a few notable exceptions, have gone into reading rather than expressing oneself nonverbally. One exception, mentioned previously, is in sensitivity training and sensory awareness. It was somewhat faddish a few years ago to participate in such activities with the hope of some generalized improvement in one's ability to express as well as to perceive. Perhaps the greatest impact was to alter the rules of interpersonal communication and encourage some kinds of behavior that previously or in other settings were socially discouraged, such as touching, hugging, crying openly, and so on. Long before this approach, of course, we had special schools, such as the finishing schools or charm schools. The purpose of these schools was to teach young ladies how to express themselves properly and effectively in the mold of a sweet young thing. This seems old fashioned these days, but something like these schools might make a comeback as our interest in the nonverbal sector increases. Then there are the courses or programs in speech, which always have included some attention to the nonverbal ("don't lean on the podium"; "stop jingling the coins in your pocket"; "use bigger gestures"; and so on. A beginning student of public speaking is typically more concerned about his or her nonverbal behavior than with the speech itself—fears of looking nervous or worries about what to do with one's hands. And certainly many public speakers do seem oddly disjointed in comparing their movements with their speeches. It is also worth mentioning that very few courses in foreign language give any mention to the particular nonverbal behaviors that normally accompany the speaking of that language. (Only one bilingual dictionary attempts to list the meanings of gestures; not surprisingly, it is an Italian-English dictionary.)

There are, however, at least two fields that have given more attention to expression than to reception or reading. One of these is the clothing industry and the peripheral figures, such as the designers, the critics like those who pick the ten best and ten worst dressed men and women each year, the beauticians who decide on the appropriate makeup, and so on. The second field that comes to mind is that of design, including architecture and interior design.

A few years ago *Time* magazine featured an article on John T. Molloy, who gives professional advice on how to dress to achieve specific results. His clients have included trial lawyers, salesmen, corporate recruiters, and others. *Time* reports that Molloy once hired an actor to pose as a trainee in a New York City corporate office. The actor was instructed to try to get secretaries to give him special information from their files.

> First the actor dressed in "lower-middle-class" style: black shoes with large buckles, a greenish-blue suit, a white shirt and a chintzy blue polyester tie, thick glasses and a gold expansion watch band. In that garb he was able to get only twelve secretaries out of 50 to go to the files for him. Later, in an "upper-middle-class" outfit—styled hair, expensive blue suit, beige shirt, silk polka-dot tie and brown cordovan shoes—he visited 50 more secretaries. This time, 42 of the 50 did as they were bade.[11]

Or so Molloy tells it.

[11] "The Groomer," *Time* (September 4, 1972), p. 39.

Clothing, makeup, and hair styling are quite similar in that they can be altered radically and easily, serve as symbols of identification of an age group (and an age), are bolstered by a large commercial market that constantly draws attention to them and often attempts to sell products by making people nervous about their own clothing, hair, or makeup. They serve to form "first impressions more, probably, than most other aspects of nonverbal behavior, such as facial expressions and gestures, and remain more or less unchanged during the course of some segment of communication. Crack trial lawyers are known to advise their clients on how to dress and appear in order to plead their particular case, and some also admit that they sometimes accept or reject prospective jury members on the basis of their appearance. In popular myth, if not always in fact, the people most conscious of clothing and appearance are the public figures, particularly the public persuaders like lawyers, politicians, actors, actresses, and salesmen. Those assumed to be unconcerned with appearance are people who work alone or at least without regard to public acclaim—the reclusive philosopher, writer, or scientist.

If clothing with its impact on first impressions helps to define a situation, clothing and general appearance are also especially subject to anticipated definitions of situations. Parties are frequently announced as casual, come as you are, informal, or the ambiguous semiformal and formal. (The North American cultural value of informality is also likely to be reflected in the closet wardrobe.) For those people especially sensitive about such things, it is sometimes difficult to find just the right clothing for the anticipated atmosphere.

For reasons of fashion more than simple cleanliness, we assume, many people are reluctant to wear the same outfit twice in a row to the same occasion with the same people present. (This does not apply to uniforms, of course.) For to do so would seem to communicate a lack of imagination or memory, or simply a lack of clothing. Within fairly definable limits, we expect a single individual to vary this aspect of his or her nonverbal expressiveness. Quite the opposite seems to be true of facial expressions, gestures, and so on; the person who smiles differently or gesticulates in notably different ways on different occasions would be judged severely.

Some of the above comments seem especially descriptive of the straight people, so that not surprisingly those identified with the counter-culture may appear exactly the opposite; they may always wear the same clothes, for example. This choice, too, serves as a means of identification with that group and at the same time as a means of distinguishing themselves from the establishment types.

Much that we have said about clothing can also be said of our surroundings, the rooms and other settings in which interpersonal communication occurs and which exert influences on that communication. Rooms and their furnishings are also prepared in advance, remain largely unchanged during the course of a segment of communication, serve as symbols of identification for the owner or host, and often help to define the situation for those who enter it. There have now been many studies of the apparent influences of some rooms on interpersonal communication, and most seem to confirm what we would expect—that the setting makes a difference. In a pair of famous studies comparing a "beautiful room" and an "ugly room" on apparently unrelated discussions that went on in the rooms, those in the unattractive setting later reported feelings of greater fatigue, irritation, and relief upon leaving.[12]

The arrangement of furniture, too, influences communication. In some settings in some societies instead of chairs there will be small stools or cushions, which are easily moved around and which naturally place the individual close to the floor giving a greater sense of space above. In other settings rooms will be heavy with massive chairs, tables, overstuffed sofas, and the like, which cannot be moved. The reciprocal influence of furniture design and placement and the patterns of proxemics of the culture or group become apparent through experience and have been studied empirically. Professional interior designers, especially those designers of commercial establishments such as hotel lobbies, restaurants, bars, and lounges, are particularly aware of the impact of furnishings on the kind of communication that will

---

[12] A. H. Maslow and N. L. Mintz, "Effects of Esthetic Surroundings: I. Initial Effects of Three Esthetic Conditions Upon Perceiving 'Energy,' and 'Well Being' in Faces," *Journal of Psychology*, 41 (1956), pp. 247–254; N. L. Mintz, "Effects of Esthetic Surroundings: II Prolonged and Repeated Experience in a 'Beautiful' and 'Ugly' Room," *Journal of Psychology*, 41 (1956), 459–466; both included in *Interpersonal Communication: Survey and Studies*, ed. Dean C. Barnlund (Boston: Houghton Mifflin, 1968), pp. 543–557.

take place. If you can think of some setting where communication seems especially easy and pleasant, or especially awkward and discomforting, you might look again at the arrangement of the furniture as a first clue for the influence.

The fixed character of furniture and other furnishings in a setting has several influences on interpersonal communication. Often the setting and arrangement impose their own definition of the larger situation, which facilitates or hampers certain kinds of communication. Library reference rooms allow many people to be together, but also exude an influence for each person to be alone and not talk to others. A singles bar is intended for the opposite purpose. But it is possible to work within the setting and pick up a date in the reference room, or to be alone in a singles bar. A young man in a singles bar, standing alone near the door, glancing at his watch and at the door each time it opens, probably defines his situation to others in the bar as waiting for someone. A person entering the library reference room and finding most of the tables empty, save for a couple seated close together at one table, may infer that the couple are at least good friends, even though they may not be looking at each other or talking together.

Many years ago a student pointed out a similar effect for dating couples riding in a car. The driver, of course, is obliged to sit more or less behind the wheel. Assuming the driver is the man, on a first date his girl may for some time sit close to her door. As their relationship becomes warmer or more intimate, she is expected to move closer and closer to her boyfriend. If there is an argument, she may slide back over to her door. But, as the student pointed out, once the couple is married for even a short period of time, the wife is again expected to sit closer to the door and not right next to her husband. Because a car is both private and public, the spatial arrangement of the couple serves to define the situation both for themselves and for outsiders. Hence the quip of friends when seeing a romantic couple sitting far apart, "Look at them. They're acting like they're married already!"

Also note the influence of the car design on the communication within. If a person is of sufficient status to have his or her own driver, the high-status person may be expected to ride in the back seat of the car and not up next to the driver. Cultural values enter into this picture, as well as economics and pure custom; in many societies where ranking and status are emphasized, we find many more single backseat passengers than we do in the United States, where the values produce more symmetrical relationships.

Apart from this, if you have a car with four or five persons inside, it is often difficult to maintain a single conversation. Eye contact is limited because of the automobile design, and additional noise from driving makes conversation difficult. Among good friends, separate conversations are likely to develop among those who can speak to each other most easily. But if the four or five people are relative strangers and wish to be polite, there may be some pressure to try to maintain a single conversation, involving everybody, which can be awkward. (So far as I know, very little study has been done of communication in cars, which is odd, considering how much time Americans spend conversing in cars.)

Although the automobile provides one of the clearest examples of the imposition of the setting and seating, other examples such as booths, long sofas, and banquet tables can be recalled as well. Often when one is stuck with furniture that he can neither arrange nor avoid, the person is then also stuck with whomever he or she happens to be seated next to. On the other hand, if one enters a setting where one has a choice of seating or can move the chairs for seating, one has greater freedom to use the furniture as an aid in communication and also as a sign of the definition of the situation.

We seem to have the least freedom of movement and interpersonal orientation when seated on fixed or heavy furniture, the most freedom when standing and talking. But most of our talking over any length of time is done while seated. When we have a choice of seating, a major consideration in our choice is that of eye contact. This aspect of the "nonverbal" area has been studied considerably in the past two decades. Although we will not go into details of any of the studies, for there are many factors and variables, at least we should recognize what some of these factors seem to be. One of the first to note is that of cultural or subcultural influence; how and to what extent two people look at each other during some segment of interaction is very much a product of their cultural background. We learn how and when to look. The teacher scolding a pupil and saying, "Look at me, I'm talking to you!" is reflecting the teacher's own cultural influence and the norms of looking to show respect and to show that one is listening. A Japanese teacher, traditionally, might expect the opposite: "Don't look at me, I'm talking to you. Looking down or looking at the point of the knot in a teacher's necktie is a Japanese norm of respectful listening. But we needn't go to Japan to find such variations. Inner-city blacks who are rapping tend to look down more than inner-city whites. Looking into the eyes of another is more likely to be a signal of anger or contempt among some groups. Similar variations have been noted among other ethnic groups, including some North American Indians. In any case, eye contact during interpersonal communication is to a considerable extent a learned behavior, like speech.

The degree of intimacy and alienation is also a factor in eye contact, which is not surprising because this can also be said of practically every other aspect of interpersonal communication. Lovers can make eyes at each other for relatively long periods of time; a stranger who does so may frighten another. Almost any perceived difference between interacting people also makes a difference, again apparently a general rule for most categories considered in verbal and nonverbal interpersonal communication. Thus the older with the younger, blacks with whites, males with females, and so on tend to reduce eye contact unless these people are already friendly or, of course, related.

There are other factors, which are more related to the content of the speaking. If people are friendly or quarreling, joking or trying to solve a difficult problem, their eye interaction will reflect this. It has been observed that when a group is pondering a rather abstract or profound question, there is a tendency to move back from one another and sometimes to stare into the air—as if the answer to such an abstract question is floating around somewhere. When they start to "zero in" or "get down to business" on a matter—and the metaphors are revealing—they tend to move closer, look down more, and look more at each other. Looking at another also serves to signal that one expects the other to speak, or at least nod agreement or disagreement, or acknowledge understanding. Much of our eye interaction in interpersonal communication is of this regulatory kind.

Even before scholars started to study patterns of eye contact in interpersonal encounters, psychologists had begun studies of physiological reactions in the eyes to certain stimuli. It has long been noted that the pupils of our eyes dilate, or expand, when viewing something pleasant or favorable and constrict when viewing something we do not like.[13] Naturally, what makes one person's eyes dilate may make another's constrict, such as when two people of different political persuasions view pictures of various political figures. This sort of reaction occurs even when the stimulus is below the conscious threshold of the viewer, as in experiments where slides are flashed on a screen at a high speed so that the viewer cannot say what he or she saw. For the psychologists conducting these experiments, a special camera can record these changes. But more important, in interpersonal encounters other people can also sense widening and narrowing of the pupils. Perhaps this is the reason that many expressions in many languages throughout the world remark that the eyes are "the windows of the soul."

A Backward Glance

Sometimes the history of studying communication seems backward. For a couple of thousand years communication, or rhetoric, was concerned almost exclusively with speaking, particularly with speeches of identifiably important people, who were consciously attempting to persuade a given audience. Only recently has there been any general effort in the field to study interpersonal communication; and even this began with unusual groups—either decision-making or task groups, or groups that came together in order to discuss their discussing. The concern for the nonverbal factors in ordinary interpersonal communication is a very recent activity, even though it appears that the majority of what is communicated is within this area. Its current place in our understanding of communication is reflected, it seems to me, in the use of the word *nonverbal*, suggesting that the verbal is still the norm or standard and the nonverbal is everything else. If so, everything else seems to include almost everything.

[13] Eckhard Hess and James Polt, "Pupil Size As Related to Interest Value of Visual Stimuli," *Science*, 132 (1960), pp. 349–350.

SIX

ON MODELS
AND METAPHORS

Trying to understand something as complex as communication often leads to choosing one of two routes: breaking it down into small parts (analysis) and studying in depth one or more of those parts; or, trying to see things as a whole, which necessarily entails looking at other related phenomena and studies of such phenomena. People sometimes describe the first as "narrow and deep," and the other as "broad but shallow." By extension the two routes describe the paths of the proverbial specialist and generalist, the former learns more and more about less and less until he eventually knows everything about nothing, while the other learns less and less about more and more until he eventually knows nothing about everything.

There is also a middle path (there always is), which is at least as familiar to most of us in daily life as it is to scholars. This is the choice to find something simpler or more familiar than a complicated subject of study, but which seems to resemble a complex matter. In academic circles, those identified with the social sciences may speak of using models; those identified with the humanities may speak of metaphors. The principle is similar and it may be that, as some writers have argued, most social science models really are closer to metaphors anyway. Following the logic of all of this, it should be easier for us to understand the idea of a model by looking at a simple model, such as a child's model airplane. It resembles a real plane in some ways—its shape, or structure and the relationship of its parts; but it is simpler, having many fewer parts, and is obviously smaller in scale. We can learn something about real planes by studying models, and if we were in the aerospace industry, we would probably build many models before actually building the real plane

The case for metaphors is somewhat different. Our everyday speech is rich with metaphoric expressions, which liken one thing to something else. Often, particularly in fresh metaphors, we speak of abstract or very complicated subjects in a language of concrete, more specific realities. Our treatment of time is an interesting example. The phenomenon of time is very complicated to understand, as philosophers and scientists have discovered over the centuries, but we talk about time in rather simple metaphors. In English we seem to use two metaphors most often. In one set, time is catching up, will pass up by, waits for no man, and so on; time is like something animate that is racing with us, a race we will eventually lose. But in another set of expressions, time is quite different. Time can be saved, wasted, budgeted, earned, lost, and so on, as if time were like money. The first set seems to be the older; the latter emerged only about two hundred years ago. We may wonder if it makes a difference how we talk about time—since the comparisons are so different, one beyond the control of man, the other within human control. In any case, we do use these two metaphors as ways of symbolically dealing with the abstract notion of time.

Then, dear philosopher, what is life? Life is a dream, a dance, a struggle, a search, or a gamble. Authors, poets, and playwrights have presented life through different metaphors at different times—a wasteland, a labyrinth, a brothel, a mental institution, a zoo, a cabaret. And more than one critic has remarked that *only* such metaphors can compress the human condition into manageable, meaningful form. The poet or playwright, obviously, must seek to discover or invent the metaphor that best expresses his or her interpretation of life. The tired (but not quite dead) metaphors of everyday speech—like "budget your time"—are used without much awareness of their "as if" quality, though they are equally imaginative.

What about interpersonal communication? What models or metaphors might we invent? What might we choose among those that have been suggested already? Indeed, what elements of metaphors are already built into the language of interpersonal communication?

If you were to look at almost any book on interpersonal communication written in the past ten years or so, you would probably find these terms used frequently: role, setting, act, action, back stage, front stage, dialogue, performance, encoding, decoding, sender, receiver, channel, feedback, processing of data, and noise.

It is not too unusual these days to find all of these terms included in the same book or even in the same theory. But even if mixed metaphors pass unnoticed these days, both the source for the metaphors and the relatedness of the terms should be recognized. The first set comes out of drama—out of drama and into early sociology and psychology. The second set comes from games and gambling—out of games and gambling and into mathematics and political science and even into pop psychology. The third set obviously comes out of cybernetics or computer technology—out of the computer lab and into early communication theory. Each seems to have its appropriateness and also its inappropriateness. In communicating we are not exactly— performing little dramas, playing games with each other, or processing information. But if we think for awhile in these terms, or as if we were, we may gain some new insights. We will begin with the oldest, the drama.

The Dramatic Metaphor

All over the world and throughout time, it seems, children in the process of growing up have acted out little plays.[1] They play house, or store, or war, or hospital. Even a child alone frequently enters into a little imagined as-if world of adults. And for adults, too, the drama as bound to ritual appears to be the oldest expressive form. By all of the grand justifications of relevance—historically, anthropologically, sociologically, religiously—it would be hard to find a form of human expression as ancient, as universal, or as essential as the drama.

[1] Susanna Miller, *The Psychology of Play* (Middlesex, England and Baltimore: Penguin Books, 1968).

But back to the scene of neighborhood children playing. What characterizes their play? What features are essential? A sense of a setting impresses us; even young children have a sense of where the drama is to take place and what is outside their area, although they may not mark off the area. And there are performers or actors; the children take on certain roles. One child may play several roles, or just a single role—on a raft afloat in the ocean. The roles tend to be types, what adults might call stock characters—the customer, the policeman, whatever—identified with professions or with temporary conditions, such as the lost boy. Often props—a stick, mud balls, a chair—will be used, and often bits of costume will be added, though these seem less essential. If you watch children at play you will also be impressed by a sense of timing; their drama begins and they bring it to an end at a point in time. If mother calls them home or tells them to clean up the room, they may quickly add a final performance to bring things to an end—"then the flood came and everybody died." There is some direction, though not always a single director—unless it is the initiator of the play or a bossy child. An outside audience is not important; the players are their own audience. A curtain, tickets, and the like associated with commercial drama will be used, we may note, only when there is an invited audience and a very clear division between audience, audience area, actors, and stage.

We may find that these characteristics of the simplest sort of children's drama will suit us very well in describing at least some kinds of interpersonal communication. We seem to have everything we might need save for one important element—plot or story line, the sequence of actions that seems fundamental to any concept of a drama. Where does this come from? If we think carefully we see that in one sense, at least the plot has already been determined: given (as roles) a mother, a sad boy, the man at the candy store, and the burglar; given (as setting) a poor house in the city; given the opening scene with the little boy crying. We have already implied the plot—or at least much of it. But what about that robber. Is he a really mean guy or a kind Robin Hood? Will he rob from the candy seller or take candy from the baby? That will depend . . . for perhaps, or even probably, the children don't quite know when the play begins. The more we know about what movies and television programs the children watch, what books they read, what sort of social background they come from, what their mother or father does to earn money, the better we are at guessing. But we don't know for sure, and probably they don't either. That's what makes the play fun. And, perhaps, that's life.

If we turn from the children's play to the terminology of the drama, we should note some interesting functional ambiguities in the language of drama, which help to explain the dynamics of the drama and the dramatic metaphor for communication. We will consider only three aspects.

1. Act. Out of context *act* has several potential meanings. It is a verb—"act right away," a term for movement. As a noun it gathers into *action*, including a collective *action* of a group performance—"the action seemed slow." Act is also a collective word for all actions in a particular sequence, which are demarcated, segmented from other actions (Act I, Act II, and Act III). *To act* also means to pretend—"he was just acting sick," meaning he really wasn't sick. We might also say that we are most aware of something as only acting when the acting is not particularly good. And by implication it is impossible to tell a really good act from reality.

2. Role. Role is also more ambiguous than it might at first appear. Some roles are temporary, relative to somebody else—"I had the role of taking notes at the meeting," or "the role of the listener" in contrast to one who is speaking. But there are also roles that are similar to professions, or occupations, or specialized functions over a long period of time, such as the role of mother or the role of a teacher. Borrowing directly from the dramatic influence we also speak of personalities in terms of roles—the role of the villain, the role of the hero, or the role of the scapegoat or patsy.

3. Setting is less ambiguous, but it includes time as well as place, and general as well as specific times and places. Note the change of mood as each new element of this setting is described: midnight, under a full moon, in an abandoned house, in 1890, in Transylvania. . . ." Guess who's coming to dinner?

In ordinary language these terms are, as noted, ambiguous, but functionally so. That is, it seems closer to reality as we experience it to think of an act as a single movement, as a larger unit of action, as an outward expression, and as containing the possibility of pretense. And so on with role, setting, and other terms we could list.

Our ordinary language provides us with an unstated logic of relationships that may serve us better than any new terms and definitions that would be free of ambiguities. Kenneth Burke has said much the same things about his dramatistic approach in which he seeks not to avoid ambiguities, but to locate those points where ambiguities are most likely to arise. [2]

If "life is a stage," if most interpersonal communication can be best understood and described as if it were a drama, then perhaps we can best learn about interpersonal communication by studying drama. This is a possibility that should not be abandoned in a race to make a science of the study of communication. It is no accident—or maybe it is—that so many courses in interpersonal communication are allied with courses in drama, or in the oral interpretations of literature in speech departments. It is only unfortunate that his marriage admits impediments.

Be that as it may, there are two theorists who have made much of the dramatic metaphor for the analysis of interpersonal communication on both a small and a grand scale. The small scale theorist is Erving Goffman; the grand explicator, Kenneth Burke.

As Goffman Sees It

Erving Goffman has his credentials as a sociologist in the tradition of other role theory sociologists. [3] But there is a difference. Whereas some of his colleagues write in a kind of Latin physics with formulae, statistical data, and chart the progress of great social movements (race relations, marriage and family, social mobility, and so on), Goffman has

[2] Kenneth Burke, A Grammar of Motives (New York: Prentice Hall, 1945), p. xx.

[3] For a discussion of Goffman's place in the sociological tradition of role theory, see Morton Deutsch and Robert Krauss, Theories in Social Psychology (New York: Basic Books, Inc., 1965), pp. 203–211.

stayed mostly within the confines of the dramatic metaphor, providing a point of view more clearly than a system. He is interested in such matters as how two strangers who find themselves walking side by side will instinctively change their pace so that one falls behind; how drivers at filling stations often feel free to walk into the shop, rummage through parts, and use the toilet as if they were at home; how people behave to express to others that they are waiting for someone. The little performances of everyday life. From his critics he has received this compliment: Goffman would have made a great novelist.

Goffman's basic approach is something like this. Whenever people encounter each other, some "definition of that situation" will be imposed by one or more of the participants. And this definition will both reflect and serve to guide the kind of behavior we can expect thereafter.[4] A policeman approaching a street quarrel, for example, must impose his definition of that situation—his authority moving in on a public disturbance. The policeman is aided in his performance by his uniform, manner, facial expressions, and so on, and in the United States probably by his physical size as well. Cops, like stewardesses, have to meet physical qualifications to enable them to join the force. Not all people can readily dramatize their role or their relationship in a given situation.

Some performances are easier to dramatize ("dramatic realization," in Goffman's terms) than others. The teacher can try to dramatize his role, however he or she conceives of it, more easily than the student. Students can dramatize their role perhaps best during final examination week, when baggy clothes, and baggy eyes and often calculated fatigue are vividly expressed. A doctor of medicine can realize his dramatic performance far better than a doctor of philosophy, because the medical doctor has his white gown and paraphernalia that impress his audience. (Little wonder an operating room is often called a theatre.) Nurses, Goffman points out, sometimes have little to do but perform some tasks—swishing around with clipboards, taking temperatures, and so on—in order to dramatize to their poor audiences that they are doing their best to help cure the patients.

In these and other performances often the values and expectations

[4] The approach described here is from Goffman's first book, *The Presentation of Self in Everyday Life* (Garden City: Doubleday Anchor, 1959).

of society at large will be best idealized. Again the obvious but important observation by Goffman that a person's behavior in the presence of others will tend to "exemplify and incorporate the officially accredited values of the society" much more than does that person's behavior when alone or when considered as a whole.[5] This means that the person may act in ways he or she does not really feel, but rather feels compelled by social pressure or social expectations. In the past, perhaps especially in the South, a bright young woman might have to conceal her intelligence so as not to embarrass the gentleman caller and to appear "ladylike." The writings from any of the liberation movements—black power, student power, women's lib, red power, and so on—are filled with examples of having to act one way because of social expectations or prejudices when the individual would have perferred to act another way. For example, there is the image of the itinerant black man who, when brought before the judge, shuffles to convey an impression of harmless, dull wit. Off stage, out of court and among friends, his behavior may change.

Goffman also notes that it may be necessary to "dramatize" that one had ideal motives or qualifications for whatever one is doing or wishes to do. Many prospective college students are required to submit, as part of their application form, a brief essay on "Why I Wish to Come to Boola U." And most know that reasons like "it's the easiest school," or "my girl friend goes there," or "the tuition is cheap and I can live at home," are not as good reasons as "because of its diversity of students, well balanced liberal arts curriculum, and excellence in the field I wish to major in."

Goffman's treatment of performances is similar to Aristotle's classical notion of rhetoric or persuasion—to artistically use the symbols and symbolic actions at hand to convey a particular impression. And so even if one does not have advantages of a particular costume or uniform or other outward signs of his or her role, the person can still, through his "personal front" and "manner" (Goffman's terms), perform as necessary. Out of character there may be little to distinguish a hard-sell car salesman from a soft-sell salesman or, for that matter, from the company's accountant or a customer. But in action—the differences become apparent.

[5] Ibid., p. 35.

Goffman in his early work expresses concern for the "cycle of disbelief to belief," as he talks about the range of performances from sincere (where one really believes in the performance, indeed does not feel he is acting) to cynical (where its all an act).[6] Americans are likely to associate cynical performances with used car salesmen, encyclopedia salesmen, real estate agents, many politicians, undertakers, and, of course, most of the marginal or illegal trades, such as confidence men, prostitutes, and phony stock salesmen. And Goffman draws upon the successfully proven performances of such characters in order to find clues about the more sincere performances. As with the ambiguities of dramatic terms mentioned before, it is often difficult to distinguish a sincere performance from a cynical one, or to assume that what begins as a cynical performance will end as one. If a teacher praises a student for work the teacher does not think is so great, but does so because the teacher thinks the student needs a boost in morale, is that sincere or cynical? What of the student who can't finish a term paper on time and tells the teacher that he is sick ("ill," as the note from home might say). Is that a cynical performance? But suppose the student does not want to thoroughly deceive the teacher—that is not part of his self-concept, let us assume—and so the student comes to feel at least a little bit sick; then what starts out as insincere ends unexpectedly sincere. Or better yet, the raw recruit in the army who "can't take all this crap" involved in basic training, but goes through the motions because he has to, not because he thinks it makes any difference. Later he may come to believe that he has been molded into the very model of a modern major.

But it is the other part of the act, the active part, that most occupies Goffman's attention with the "dramaturgical" model. From the drama he borrows the terms *front stage* and *backstage*, and applies them very much as they are used in drama. The front stage is where one appears before the audience and is conscious of the audience; it is here that the performance takes place. Backstage, amidst the props, ropes, and actors waiting in the wings, a performer can relax and act out of character. The regions of a home or building have their front and backstage areas, the parts where visitors are entertained and the parts where only the members of the family may go. When company

[6] Ibid., pp. 17–22.

comes, usually only part of the house is cleaned up and prepared for the visit; the comic books, green stamp catalogue, and trashy novel are tossed backstage, replaced by the kind of book Mark Twain called a classic, a book praised but not read. For some guests, children may be shunted off backstage for fear they might not perform well or, indeed, might even spoil the performance the host and hostess wish to make. If this all sounds like a very middle-class sort of performance, it need not be so limited.

The "total performance" idea leads to a basic theme in Goffman. By mixing his metaphor slightly, he introduces the concept of *teams*. There are performer teams and audience teams; there are also outsiders who don't fit either category, such as grandma who sits hunched in her chair to be ignored like a piece of furniture, or the guest left alone in the living room while the host or hostess leaves to answer the door. But the idea of teams is basic to Goffman's scheme, as he points out that without such a concept we can misunderstand and overlook most of the important elements of our performances.[7]

Many, perhaps most, performances are not solo acts. Even those which sometimes seem to be, such as the private interview, often employ a supporting cast of secretaries, receptionists, assistants, and so on, who help to carry off the performance. There are also some professional variations of individual or team performances. In the past, at least, Roman Catholic nuns would always travel in pairs or larger groups; party hosts or hostesses often involve others, even newly arrived guests; firemen rarely work individually. Goffman speculates that most blue-collar workers spend most of their work time in relatively large teams, while executives work backstage in smaller and smaller teams as their rank and power increases. We could also note cultural differences, which derive from both cultural values and conventions. The Japanese, for example, almost never appears alone; businessmen travel in pairs or groups, vacations are usually taken in groups, even some honeymoons are group affairs.

For Goffman "any set of individuals who cooperate in staging a single routine" constitute a performance team.[8] Two fairly obvious but important features of such a relationship follow: (1) any member of a

[7] Ibid., pp. 77–105.
[8] Ibid., p. 79.

team has a kind of power to "give the show away" during the performance; and (2) to the extent that the team must cooperate to present a desired impression (or impose their definition of the situation) on the audience, they are not, individually, in any position to maintain that image when they are off stage. It follows that members of the team who may disagree or even dislike each other personally will have to hide such differences when before others. In the harried moments before guests arrive, a husband and wife may be running around and shouting at each other; but when the guests arrive at the door, the couple becomes as one in their performance. And should some gross error or indiscretion be committed by one of the team members during a performance, the others may have to cover up for that person; "I think that what Mike *meant* was. . . ." Such confusions are often a stock situation in comedies. Goffman also notes that sometimes in addition to selecting teammates who express the right image for the performances (stewardesses, receptionists for major corporations, the Playboy bunny, and so on), people will be selected because they can be trusted to perform properly.

Dividing people into "performance teams" and "audience teams" is helpful, though sometimes the distinction is blurred or changes over a period of time. Goffman makes the distinction on the basis of who manages the setting—the host of a party is on the performance team, the guests, the audience team. But taking the case of a party at somebody's home, it is possible that a host may give a party in order to impress some of the guests, and may be very selective in inviting people who will most impress each other and, hence, make the host look good. In such a case, it is hard to say who is on whose team simply on the basis of controlling the setting. To vary the maxim, we may judge a person by the company he invites.

Several years ago in a Chicago suburb a restaurant began to offer a special service to customers who wanted to use the restaurant to impress guests. If a young college man wanted to impress a girl he hoped to date, he could telephone the restaurant in advance and make arrangements to prepare the scene. When he and his date arrived at the restaurant, even if he had never been there before, he would be treated like an old, familiar customer. "Good evening, Mr. Brown. Would you like your usual table? Which of the wines in your private stock would you like with your meal?" A cynical performance indeed, but one of a variety of kinds of performances in which a person who appears to be on one team actually is working for another team. Goffman identifies several kinds of double roles, but we need consider only three.

1. The informer. Images of the CIA agent, undercover narcotics agents, the FBI, NKVD, and all the other secretive organizations, which comprise much of the popular literature of the past three decades. Members of congressional committees or people in high positions who leak information to reporters, such as the mysterious Deep Throat in Bernstein and Woodward's exposé of the Watergate business.[9] And so can a good many social science researchers, particularly the participant-observer kind who join a company, gang or hospital ward in order to discover information and later report it. (Gloria Steinem's first big story was her exposé of the Playboy bunny, written after having been employed for a time as a bunny.)

Here perhaps moral judgments should be avoided, but it is interesting that some of the people in these "discrepant roles," as Goffman calls them, are praised—the modern muckraker, like Jack Anderson, the vigorous investigative reporter. Sociologists, too, are double agents for the advancement of knowledge, it is said. But political spies seem to be despised by the government they work for as well as against and, apparently, are often pressed into service for less than noble reasons (through blackmail or promises of certain rewards). Even Moses got the word that bearing false witness was one of the ten great mortal sins.

2. The shil. Just off stage, often at the sideshow, is the carnival shil. The shil is the person who appears to be a member of the audience, but, in fact, is working for the troupe. He is the one who buys the ticket to go into the tent and hence hopes to draw others who don't want to be the first; he is the one who is first to buy the snake-oil, the first to walk down the sawdust trail, the first to bid at the big city auction that sells schlock merchandise. He is also the opera claque who shouts "bravo" at the right time for his favored performer. In some countries he may be a hired mourner at a funeral. Most seem to be cynical performances, but fans of a rock group or even parents ap-

[9] Robert Woodward and Carl Bernstein, *All the President's Men* (New York: Simon and Schuster, 1974).

plauding their child in a recital or sending in their cards and letters to support their friend in a talent contest are also shils, though somewhat more sincere.

3. The go-between. Go-betweens take many forms, and in some cultures almost no important transaction is completed without one. In the United States, the majority values tend to denigrate the role of a go-between—"speak for yourself, John"—but, as Phillipsen found in his study of communication in the heart of Chicago, go-betweens were essential in getting jobs—particularly a job connected with city politics.[10] There are famous go-betweens, such as Secretary of State Henry Kissinger and his shuttle diplomacy in negotiating a political settlement; others are practically nameless—the contact, the friend of a friend, the guide or interpreter, or translator. One characteristic of the go-between, Goffman notes, is that the go-between is often required to give the impression that he or she is more loyal to one side than the other (whichever side the go-between is talking to at the time). But there are problems of secrecy sometimes, in having said one thing to one party but not wanting to have the other party hear it. As Goffman mentions, unless one looks at the full situation in which a go-between operates, including both sets of teams, the go-between's behavior seems erratic, even bizarre.[11]

One of the most useful tips on observing interpersonal communication to come from Goffman is that to discover how things should be (as good performances) we should notice what happens when things go wrong. There may be only a split second of confusion or embarrassed silence, but in that moment much might be revealed. Examples might be when the learned authority forgets the point he was about to make; when the wise and gentle family counselor is intruded upon by his own bratty children; when, as used to happen occasionally when most television programs were done live, the advertised, new car or refrigerator didn't work. For the performer these can be terribly embarrassing. For the audience these incidents can be amusing. For the student of communication these can be more revealing than a perfect performance.

[10] Phillipsen, "Speaking 'Like a Man' in Teamsterville," *The Quarterly Journal of Speech* Vol. 61, No. 1 (Feb. 1975) pp. 13–22.
[11] Goffman, *The Presentation of Self in Everyday Life*, op. cit.

It is interesting that much of what Goffman describes when the performance goes wrong is the basis for our sense of the comic. Some time ago a group of British jokesters attended a political rally in which the politician spoke from the rear of the last car of the train—much like the old whistlestop tour in the States. These gentlemen uncoupled the last car from the rest of the train, and so as the speaker concluded with a ringing peroration, the engine started up, and the train pulled away, leaving the poor fellow bowing to applause that turned to laughter. (Nixon's nemesis Dick Tuck once performed a similar feat. He dressed in the uniform of a trainman and halfway through a Nixon speech signaled the engineer to pull out—much to the consternation of Nixon.) Mort Sahl used to tell of a black jazz group that traveled around the world under the auspices of the State Department. Asked in one interview why they came to be such great jazz performers, the leader replied, "Well, I actually wanted to become a doctor, but when the Governor closed our schools. . . ." In Goffman's terms, the expected "idealized answer" was replaced by a more honest one.

Kenneth Burke has written of a similiar phenomenon that he calls "perspective through incongruity." [12] By placing inconsistent or incongrous elements together, the result is often new insights into the familiar. This is similar to a principle of surrealistic art in which the commonplace—a dresser with drawers open, a bed, or a hat—appears in a desert scene, evoking an odd, dream-like mood and making the ordinary appear extraordianry.

Burke's Vision

I have sometimes felt that there is a difference in the general outlook toward man by scholars in the social sciences and those in the humanities. The social scientists seem particularly intrigued with problems, frustrations, and man's means of coping with them. But the poets, playwrights, and novelists, or many of them at least, seem to go beyond this to some sort of resolution, even celebration, of the humanity and dignity of man; man shall prevail. Be that as it may, the dramatic metaphor as applied by Erving Goffman and Kenneth Burke

[12] Burke, A *Grammar of Motives*, p. xvii–xxv.

differs substantially in design, goal, and most notably in the sources for illustration and evidence. Against Goffman's furniture salesman or hospital orderly, Burke will quote the trials of King Lear or Oedipus. And those who have followed the Burkeian approach into current events are most likely to look at major political figures, social movements, religious figures, rather than, say, a Burkeian analysis of a bridal shower.

Burke's dramatism, as it is often called, consists of five key terms, "the pentad." [13] At first glance these seem surprisingly familiar. Not only do they echo some terms from drama, but they are also similar to the watchwords of the journalist or of a mass media theorist like Lasswell. [14] For Burke, all questions of interpreting what we would call interpersonal communication must consider these five questions identified by the five terms of the pentad. These terms, and the questions they refer to, are

1. Act: What was done?
2. Scene: When or where did the act take place?
3. Agent: Who performed the act?
4. Agency: How was the act performed?
5. Purpose: Why was the act performed?

Although over the centuries, men have shown great enterprise and inventiveness in pondering matters of human motivation, one can simplify the subject by this pentad of key terms, which are understandable almost at a glance. They need never to be abandoned, since all statements that assign motives can be shown to arise out of them and to terminate in them. [15]

A grand design, indeed.

A good reporter is taught in journalism school to ask similar questions in getting the full story: who, what, where, when, and why. But while the journalist, at least in the old school, would want the answers to be factual, direct, and complete if itemized, the Burkeian analyst

[13] Ibid., p. xvii–xxv.

[14] Harold D. Lasswell, "The Structure and Function of Communication in Society," in *The Communication of Ideas* (Lyman Bryson, ed.). (New York: Harper and Row, 1948), p. 37.

[15] Burke, *A Grammar of Motives*, pp. xvii–xviii.

only begins with these terms. Moreover, while a reporter may feel obliged to give the lowest priority to the *why*, because that is so often in the realm of inference or speculation, for the Burkeian analyst the *why* is the most important. Burke's two best known book titles make this focus clear—*A Grammar of Motives* and *A Rhetoric of Motives*. [16] One other difference in emphasis between the Burkeian analyst and the journalist should be noted. The reporter, at least in writing a straight news story, can treat these questions as more or less independent. "Harriet Jefferson was murdered. The murder weapon was a knife. The murder occurred in the kitchen last night. The accused is her husband, and his motive appears to be jealousy." But things are not so happenstance for Burke. There are important relationships, "ratios" he calls them, among these terms, and it is in examining those ratios that motivation is most likely to be revealed and wise interpretation revealed. Consider for a moment, the remarkable event of Richard Nixon's fall from power. Some might hear vague echoes of King Lear—stripped of power, his perquisites, his retinue, and hospitalized "near death," his spokesman said. But focus on one key element in that modern tragedy, if that is what it is—the act that precipitated his fall. A Burkeian analysis might go something like this:

1. Act: The President deceived the public and failed in his sworn responsibilities.
2. Scene: The Oval Office of the White House.
3. Agent: Nixon himself.
4. Agency: A little Sony tape recorder.
5. Purpose: . . . .

It is that purpose that has most intrigued the political analysts and even some psychoanalysts. Why did he tape his own incriminating conversations? Or why didn't he destroy the tapes at the first sign of trouble? A Burkeian analysis says that we should be better able to understand such questions by looking at the ratios or relationships of the other terms. Certainly in news reports, editorials, letters to editors, and such, the terms that came up most often were "inside the Oval Office"

---

[16] Ibid; also, Kenneth Burke, A *Rhetoric of Motives* (Englewood Cliffs, N.J.: Prentice-Hall, 1950).

and "the tapes." Added to the popular semantics of the day, during the Ervin Committee hearings, was the phrase "at that point in time," suggesting that time as well as place must be regarded in such an analysis. One had the impression, in reading and observing the popular reaction to this extraordinary event, that if the conversations had not taken place in the Oval Office, but instead in a locker room or the backroom of a bar, many people would not have been so upset. Indeed, many writers referred to the expletive-deleted conversations as "locker room language," "back room political talk," and the like. It was that juxtaposition of talk and place that must be investigated.

In that analysis we might discover not only something about this extraordinary event, but also something about our feelings for the Oval Office, a room endowed with the aura of history, with dignity, and even with reverence. The mixture of sacred and profane is often upsetting and, likewise, such a reaction helps to reveal what is sacred and what is profane. It is this sort of insight that Burkeian analyses are likely to probe and reveal. For Goffman, perhaps, when the doors are closed and the president is huddled with his closest advisors, they are a team back stage. In the drama by Burkeians, I believe, backstage and front stage is too simple and insignificant a division.

The tape recorder is the agent. The president was done in not by a bullet but by a bug, by his *own* bug. An accident? A kind of suicide perhaps? But if a kind of suicide—one interpretation—then what does that agency tell us? Was it egotistical, done in by his words, strangled by his own tape? The plot thickens. Burke's pentad is at work.

One of the good things about the dramatic metaphor is that those who would apply it come from so many fields, the humanities rather more than the social sciences, and the public sphere more than from academia. (It may also be that for the same reason social scientists tend to shrug off this sort of metaphor as unhelpful.)

One of the contributions of mass media in modern society is the ironic transformation of many news events into public dramas. Sometimes it seems difficult for even a good novelist or dramatist to compete. Truth may or may not be stranger than fiction, but it is often as dramatic. A common compliment for a nonfiction work is that it "reads like a novel," thus returning the naïve compliment about drama or novels that they "seem so real!" Some of the best compromises in the fact/fiction competition in recent years have been novels based on fact, such as Truman Capote's *In Cold Blood*, and the controversial genre associated with Tom Wolfe, the new journalism, in which literary devices are at the service of journalism, or maybe vice versa. In any case it seems difficult now to separate the appeal and the style of reporting and literature, including dramatic literature. (The academic field, which produces some of the worst writing around, lags sadly behind.)

It's How You Play the Game

Play is another ubiquitous and ambiguous word in English. A drama is a play, those who participate in drama, players. "Play" connotes fun, a lack of seriousness, something easy—mere child's play. Perhaps most of all, we play games. Ball players play ball. Card players play cards. And our ordinary language is stuffed with metaphors from games, both sports and table games, particularly cards. From baseball alone we are "out in left field," "have our turn at bat," "strike out," or are "thrown a curve." All of these are sometimes said of people in the dating game, who often "play the field."

Many of the deepest American (and British) values are rooted in games. "Fair play" is often said to be one of the most difficult expressions to translate into other languages. Sportsmanship is "not whether you win or lose, it's how you play the game." Games are structured democratically. Each participant starts at the same point with an equal number of players, or cards, or chessmen for each player. Games are a perfect metaphor and a possible influence on the social values of equal opportunity, fairness, competition, and success!

The word *deal* in a political slogan (The New Deal, The Fair Deal), and in slang (a rotten deal) comes out of card games. The person who withholds information until the last minute to surprise and defeat his opponent has "an ace in the hole," or has "his trump card." The cheaters—in games or in life—use "a stacked deck," or "loaded dice."

Football, craps, and the Olympics are all games, but each has some significantly different characteristics, and if we are to apply the metaphor of the game to interpersonal communication we should be clear about these differences.

Some games resemble rituals. The Olympic games, for example, are to a great extent international rituals as well as a forum for nationalistic aggrandizement and display. And ritual is very close, as we have noted, to drama. Traditional collegiate rivalries—Harvard vs. Princeton, USC vs. UCLA—are similarly ritualistic and dramatic performances. Few sports broadcasters—whose language invariably contains many clichés—can avoid referring to "the drama" of the game, even the dullest game. Other games—especially cards, dice, horse racing (which also provides us with many metaphors)—are closely associated with gambling, and gambling adds the element of the odds, chance, luck, and winnings. Thus, taking a broad view of games we could include everything from ritual, drama, teamwork, rules, scores, probabilities, and rewards.

Little wonder, then, that the game model had been taken seriously by novelists, mathematicians, political scientists, psychologists, and people in the field of communication. Many years ago a Dutch writer, Johan Huizinga, wrote a brilliant book called *Homo Ludens*, man as the player of games.[17] Huizinga interpreted many serious institutions and procedures, such as the legal system, as if it were a game. Stephen Potter, a British humorist, wrote a series of books on human interaction as games and even his titles influenced our vocabulary a little—*One-Upmanship, Gamesmanship, Supermanship,* and so on.[18] The mathematicians, economists, and later those in political science or in "peace research," "conflict resolution," "negotiation" have joined the game model. Add the possibilities of the computer, and the game metaphor becomes more of a model than a metaphor.

Today in American colleges many students are invited to participate in games called simulations. One of the most frequently played games is that of international power politics, where students will simulate the world today or the United Nations General Assembly. One group of students will represent, for example, Argentina; another, Bolivia; another, Canada; and so on. Each will be given some basic

●

[17] Johan Huizinga, *Homo Ludens: A Study of the Play Element in Culture* (London: Routledge and Kegan Paul, 1949).

[18] See, for example, Stephen Potter, *The Theory and Practice of Gamesmanship: The Art of Winning Games Without Actually Cheating.* (New York: Holt, Rinehart and Winston, 1948).

information, as well as certain options and symbols of power. Their communications are recorded and usually fed into computers with the hope of learning something about how real governments might act in a real situation which the game is to simulate. When the activity concerns not power politics but, say, interpersonal relations in a factory, or school, or home, these simulations are more likely to be called role playing. The term reflects the dramatic metaphor. Note the similarity of the metaphors, even if the names are different.

A game, however, differs from a drama in one important respect. A game requires two or more players whose interests are at least partially and often totally in opposition—in a word, competition. (There may also be cooperation, not only by players on the same team, but in some respects between the opposing sides.) Games must have rules. In this, too, the game differs somewhat from the drama, though one could interpret many aspects of plot and keeping in character as following rules.

Although games and gambling are often related, there is a basic difference between games and some forms of gambling. To gamble with dice, roulette, a slot machine, or even a card game like black jack, each player is pitted against the odds. A well-shuffled deck no less than a well-oiled slot machine is witless; if you lose it is not because the cards or the slot machine outsmart you, it is only because the odds are against you. Thus the roulette wheel or slot machine is, in a sense, quite stupid, exceeded only in stupidity by some of the people who play against them. This points up another characteristic of games in contrast to gambles: the goal of a game is to outwit or outperform or outplay the opponent. The most serious player of a game, such as a grand master of chess, must assume that his opponent is very intelligent and will play his best. He does not hope to be lucky, or for his opponent to lapse, or even to win by bluffing. This characteristic is a vital part of the game model, though as a metaphor for life we may not want to be so strict. A hustler—Bobby Riggs, or Minnesota Fats, or one of Stephen Potter's heroes—can defeat a more skilled player by a psychological gambit, but for serious players, this is not quite in the spirit, much less the rules, of the game.

A game, then, requires two or more players whose interests are at least partially and often totally in conflict and a set of rules, which the players obey with the goal of outwitting the opponent. The question of partial or total conflict leads to a further distinction that is often basic to game theory—the zero-sum game and the nonzero-game (often symbolized as O-sum and $\overline{O}$-sum). The distinction is simple but very important. In a zero-sum game, as you might guess, the winnings and losings add up to zero. If five people play penny ante poker, and at the end of the evening you ask each how much he or she won or lost, the winnings and losses should cancel each other out. (If the house takes a cut, that's something else.) Probably when most of us think of games we think of zero-sum games because these are the most familiar for table games and sports games. But there are some games in which everybody can win or everybody can lose or, in any case, do not result in a win-lose tally of zero. A labor strike, for example, may appear to be a kind of game: labor vs. management, with labor wanting a bigger piece of the economic pie. If the strike is protracted with massive layoffs and workers off the job for some time and production at a standstill, both labor and management lose. With some settlements, both labor and management can win. With other kinds of settlements, what labor wins management seems to lose, or vice versa. Wars, too, are often compared to games and indeed there are war games, simulations of real fighting. There are wars that seem to be zero-sum games in the sense of territory captured—what country x wins, country y loses. Human casulaties seem to be of the other kind; both sides lose. A phyrric victory, one in which an army wins but at a terrible cost of material and life, is at best a mixed game.

One model of a nonzero-sum game that has attracted considerable attention as it might apply to reality is what has come to be called the prisoner's dilemma.[19] (This name seems to come from one of the old paradoxes, which appears to have no correct answer but in fact, has a subtle solution.) You are a prisoner in jail and you are told that you must say something. If what you say is true, your head will be chopped off; if what you say is false, you will be hung by the neck until dead What do you say?[20] One of the many versions of this game is as follows. There are two teams, the rows and the columns. The rows must select one of two rows, row 1 or row 2. The columns must

[19] See Anatol Rapoport, *Fights, Games and Debates* (Ann Arbor: University of Michigan Press, 1960).

[20] To win you might say, "I will be hung by my neck until dead."

	I	II
A	(+5) +5	(+10) −10
B	(−10) +10	(−5) −5

select one of two vertical columns, column A or column B. Both must make their choice simultaneously, neither knowing ahead of time what the other will choose. When their choices are announced, the combinations will determine one of four intersecting positions: A-1, A-2, B-1, or B-2. The payoff is given here with the circled numbers referring to the rows, the numbers in boxes to the columns.

The game must be played to be appreciated, and it should be played ten or twenty times in succession. What usually happens when people play this game is that over and over the result is B-2, where each side loses. Here is a game where each side *can* win, but so often both sides lose. Why? The reason is simple—or maybe not so simple. Each side is likely to play the row or column that can win the most. The rows thus select 2, the columns select B. Built into the scoring system is a bias against trusting the other side, for if the rows play 1 with the hope that the columns will play A (so that each can win), all the columns have to do is play B and win ten points while the rows lose ten points. The thoughts—and fears—of the columns work similarly. To the outsider the way to play this game seems obvious, each side should think not where it alone will profit most, but where both sides together will profit most. The ideal, then, is not an I-centered strategy, or even a you-centered strategy, but a we-centered strategy. But how is this to be proposed, encouraged, or enforced? If we let the two sides talk together and if each promises to play the we-strategy, there is still the risk that at some time—often during the last of a series of plays—one or both sides will break their promise in the interest of outscoring the opponent.

In communication classes where students have played the game, we find some interesting patterns. Some say that the real kick out of playing the game is not how many points their side wins, but rather how many points the other side loses! (David Smith has reported a similar phenomenon in a communication class many years ago at the University of Minnesota.[21] He had two rivals bidding at an auction for nickels. One side began by offering him one cent for each of his nickels; the other offered two cents; the first offered three cents and the other offered four cents; finally one offered five cents, which of course meant no profit at all. But the other side then offered six cents—in effect losing money sheerly for the pleasure of not letting the other side "win!" These examples seem to reveal a dimension of the game and life that is disturbing and difficult to treat within a simple game model, the psychological payoff, the floating, petty, nasty, narrow side of human behavior that seems so far from the model aims of sportsmanship. It's not whether you win or lose, it's how you play the game . . . so that the other side loses.

Taking just the prisoner's dilemma puzzle, we could have many people play the game over and over and see what kind of patterns emerge. We might find that there are personality, or ethnic, or even sex and age differences in preferences of play and feelings about winning or losing. We could also vary the payoffs, favoring one side slightly, or changing the nature of the rewards—symbols or forms of pleasure or pain, immediate or delayed gratifications, personal enhancement or humiliation, and so on. Many variations have been adopted into the model for experimental and illustrative purposes. But with all such games, or simulations, or role playing there is a self-consciousness of a game or an experiment, and there is no certainty that people will think of most forms of interpersonal communication games.

The game model has been applied most extensively to those situations in which conflict is central and communication takes the form of bargaining. In situations such as peace negotiations or labor-management disputes, one can be rather faithful to both the actual situation and the game model; the parties involved, the nature of the conflict, even the possible moves or strategies as well as the pay-offs, can be identified for the most part. Similarly, it is usually apparent when the game is over, winners or losers determined, and the pay-offs

[21] David Smith, personal correspondence.

made, even if such a resolution might contain the seeds of yet another conflict some time in the future. Offsetting such advantages, however, is the feeling that such clear-cut conflict situations represent a rather small percentage of our interpersonal communication behavior in daily life.

Nevertheless, there is another application of the game as metaphor which can be considered here; this is the kind represented in a best selling book on transactional psychology by Eric Berne, *Games People Play*.[22] Berne's use of the game is probably much closer to the popular notion of the relationship of games to interpersonal communication, at least as implied in such expressions as "let's stop playing games with each other" (meaning, perhaps, "let's be honest and forthright about our relationship"). In his book, Berne, a psychiatrist, described behavior he observed in his clients without using the terminology of his profession, such as "neutroic" or "disturbed." Rather, he described such behavior in terms of games with rules, strategies, psychological payoffs (such as humiliating another person or, in some cases, finding satisfaction in being humiliated). Berne also offered advice on how people could learn to stop playing such destructive games. His subject matter ran the gamut of social ills—alienation, divorce, alcoholism, and so on—but each interpersonal problem was described in terms of a communication game.

The popularity of the book suggests that quite apart from the accuracy or wisdom of Berne's observations it may have been his use of the game metaphor that was most appealing. Readers and even reviewers remarked upon how recognizeable were some of the patterns precisely because of their description as if they were games. Apart from Berne's book, there may be something appealing about the game metaphor particularly for persons engaged in certain activities. I suspect that when one is in a field that is highly competitive, where human interaction proceeds largely through verbal exchanges and symbolic manipulation (rather than physical effort) and where human relationships last only a short time, the game metaphor might seem most fitting.

We might also consider possible relationships between this view of games in interpersonal communication and what Goffman called "cynical performances," since much of what one communicates in

[22] Eric Berne, *Games People Play* (New York: Grove Press, 1964).

playing such games would be calculated for some future gain rather than a sincere expression of feelings or beliefs. We might also want to consider as games some of our compulsory, competitive activities which lead to symbolic achievements. This could include much of what passes for "education," for along with other kinds of learning many students may also learn how to play and win the term paper game, final examination game, and so on. (One can imagine another version of *Games People Play* written for students; and perhaps yet another for teachers!)

In concluding these remarks on the game as a model or metaphor for interpersonal communication, we should keep in mind that conflict is central to this view of communication. Where the nature of the conflict can be clearly stated, where rules can be established and maintained, where pay-offs are known at the outset by the players, the game model may be helpful. These characteristics may be most apparent in legal, economic, or political disputes, and it is in such fields of conflict and bargaining that game models derived from mathematical games theory have been most often applied. Through experiments and simulations we may come to learn more about the probabilities and potentials of bargaining and resolving conflicts.

There is another application of the game metaphor which lacks the precision of describing mutually agreed upon rules, strategies or even pay-offs, for the rewards of such outcomes often appear only in the minds of the players or, sometimes, in the mind of only one of the players. However, to the extent that any of us think about and talk about our activities and relationships with others as if we were playing games, this metaphor may also be revealing. Symmetrical relationships, verbal and nonverbal symbolic expressiveness, and a high value of competition coupled with the possibility of social mobility may all combine to make the game metaphor even more salient than the dramatic metaphor for certain kinds of relationships. For while we may perform to express or maintain our place in society, we may play games to put another in his place. Finally, we should consider the potential influence of the game metaphor itself only for describing interpersonal communication but as an influence on that behavior. Listen to conversations around you; listen to the ways in which you talk about dating, getting good grades, getting the right job. You may be surprised.

Vox ex Machina

The dramatic metaphor is in no way an insight of the twentieth century. Essentially, it is as old a notion as art itself. The metaphor of the game seems more recent and especially characteristic of the Anglo-American culture, particularly of the United States in this century; yet we can find comparisons of life and games elsewhere and far earlier in history. But the third model or metaphor we want to consider is very much a product of the past few decades, and in many respects this model has influenced the language and thinking of communication studies far more than either of the others. This is the influence of cybernetics, of thinking machines, of computers. Norbert Wiener, the man who coined the term *cybernetics*, lived during our lifetime.[23] Perhaps no other invention of modern times has such a potential to influence the structure and power relationships of a society. And perhaps no other metaphor has so influenced the ways in which communication scholars identify and think about interpersonal communication."

Practically anybody who studies communication, as well as many people who have not, knows of terms like *feedback, channel, noise, code, encoding, decoding, programming, information retrieval,* and *data bank.* As applied to communication, both interpersonal and technological, these are all new terms. For some scholars these are fundamental terms without which one cannot talk meaningfully about communication.

Two works, more than any others, have exerted this influence. Both were by mathematicians, both were based not on human communication but on sophisticated machines. Their premises were extended to apply to human communication. Both are regarded today as modern classics. One of these is Norbert Wiener's book *The Human Use of Human Beings;* [24] the other is *The Mathematical Theory of Communication,* [25] a combined effort by Claude Shannon and Warren

[23] Norbert Wiener died in 1964.

[24] Norbert Wiener, *The Human Use of Human Beings* (Boston: Houghton Mifflin, 1954).

[25] Clause Shannon and Warren Weaver, *The Mathematical Theory of Communication* (Urbana: University of Illinois Press, 1949).

Weaver, the former working for the Bell Telephone Company and putting forth the theory, the latter interpreting that theory in simple terms for lay readers. There is, however, an important difference between these books. The Shannon and Weaver book is a cold, clear elucidation of a theory; Wiener's book is philosophical, evocative, even passionate. It will be convenient to begin with Shannon and Weaver's contribution.

We Begin with the Naming of Parts

A communication system must contain these elements:

1. A channel, through which messages can be transmitted.
2. A sender, at one end, and a receiver, at the other.
3. A code, into which a message is converted to allow it to be transmitted.
4. An encoding device for the sender, which converts the message to the code.
5. A decoding device for the receiver, which reverses the process and turns the code back into a message.

In addition, the code is constantly threatened by distortion from without; this is called noise. But as one check against that noise and as a means of correcting distortions and making the circuit complete, there is likely to be feedback. We might note here that feedback is a central concept in Wiener's cybernetic theory and philosophy and also probably the cybernetic-related term most used by the general public.

These terms, of course, have fixed relationships with each other, which may be best seen through the graphic model.[26]

There are by now dozens of variations on this model and we do best by treating them together rather than trying to be faithful to the original by Shannon and Weaver.[27] And also, because we are interested in interpersonal, face-to-face communication rather than tele-

[26] Based on the Shannon-Weaver model, ibid., p. 98.
[27] Perhaps the best known variation of this model is that by David Berlo presented in his *The Process of Communication* (New York: Holt, Rinehart and Winston, 1960).

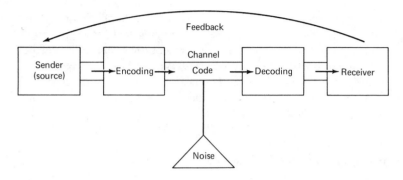

phone or television transmission, we will attempt to consider these relationships.

Starting with the term *channel*, we can ask through what channels do people communicate or participate in communication? Many writers will say that the human being is a multisensory being who uses many channels simultaneously: the auditory channel for voice, the visual channel for expression and perceiving nonverbal expressions, and even channels like the olfactory (for smell) and the thermal (for temperature). So far so good. We can now turn to questions of what channels people prefer to use, what channels are supplementary, or emergency channels, and so on. As for codes, again we have the code of spoken language, of gestures, and of the whole symbolic stuff of clothing, artifacts, interpersonal distance, and at least twenty more codes which social scientists have identified and studied. Naturally, channels and codes are related. We can not use an auditory channel for visual messages, like a hand gesture. The visual channel, however, is closely related to speech, because it is often more difficult to hear a person when you cannot see the person move his lips or gesticulate than when you can. But also note that a deaf person who can read lips can decode the same message that a hearing person senses through another channel, providing both can see and hear the same person speaking.

The process of encoding and decoding is easily illustrated and understood. A customer in a restaurant is seated at a table and wants to order. To communicate this, he encodes his intention by waving his hand, or calling to the waiter, to mention two obvious codes and their corresponding channels. If the waiter has his back turned to the customer, as is usually the case, the waiter cannot receive the wave sent through the visual channel. If the waiter sees the customer wave, but is a stupid waiter who decodes that wave as a sign of friendliness, he may smile and wave back. If so, the encoding and transmission was all right, but something went wrong with the decoding. Perhaps a more realistic example would be a simpler situation with the waiter coming over, taking the order (oral-aural), writing down the order (graphic-visual), and going to the kitchen to place the order on the cook's spindle. The cook reads this, further decodes it, performs an appropriate reaction that results in a plate of food; the cook then rings a bell for the waiter to pick up the food, the waiter picks up the plate and delivers it to our somewhat hungrier customer.

But now let's suppose that the customer says, "This is not what I ordered." Even in this abbreviated sequence of messages we can see that there are many places where the communication may have broken down. And our model should help us to identify those possibilities. A waitress friend tells me that there are many customers who either do not order what they meant to or thought they had ordered, or else they forget what they ordered. This poses a problem it is difficult for the waiter or waitress to argue with the customer—for reasons that lie outside of this particular model of communication. The problem may have originated with the original encoding, or the problem might lie with the waiter writing the wrong order, or not writing clearly, or the cook misreading what was correctly written, or reading it correctly but still preparing the wrong dish, or in the waiter delivering the "right meal" to the wrong table. This may seem to be a trivial example for such an influential theory of communication, but at least it illustrates what some of the terms represent.

We might as well continue with the same situation to illustrate the idea of noise and a partial application of feedback. In the crowded restaurant there will be noise in the usual sense of the word; other conversations and the clatter of dishes may interfere with the message going smoothly from the customer to the waiter. In this model of communication, however, the term *noise* includes any sort of interference from outside the message that threatens the faithful transmission of the message. Thus, sunlight glaring in the eyes of the waiter or even the distraction of a customer's low-cut neckline could be regarded as noise. Some noise can be used to reduce other noise. Background music or muzak, for example, is often used to smooth over conversations that might be more distracting and to tone down other sorts of distractions.

Feedback is a corrective mechanism by which the receiver communicates to the sender the information received, or part of it, to help insure that the message received was indeed the message sent. Our waiter friend is likely to repeat the order, to make sure that (1) he heard what was said, and (2) to let the customer know that he heard correctly. As a rule, the greater the risk from noise, the greater is the need for some sort of feedback; and similarly the more complicated the message, the greater the need for feedback.

So far, the application of this model does not seem so remarkable as to have had a great deal of influence on interpersonal communication theory. Indeed, it largely seems to supply new impersonal names to familiar more personal realities. Why then, all the excitement? For one thing, this model shifts the emphasis from one-way communication of the public speaker or the writer to a circular process, or rather, it was the key element of feedback that did the trick. It is now a commonplace in communication articles and books to distinguish old communication theory from new communication theory in terms of one-way versus two-way, or circular process communication.

The model may also have opened the way to a greater awareness of channels in addition to the attention given only to the spoken word until sometime in the eighteenth century and the written word until well into this century.

The model also heightened awareness of how and where communication can break down. That is, while Caesars and emperors throughout history have been concerned with breakdowns in lines of communication from the center to more remote areas, it was most unusual to think of communication breaking down in the process of people talking to one another. The emphasis historically has been on the speaker (or writer), who in this model is identified as the sender. This model, however, distributes the responsibility equally and impersonally among sender, receiver, channel, and so on. This is not surprising because the model was designed with the telephone in mind.

Implicit in this new emphasis is a change in norms by which communication is judged as good or bad. In this model, as with the telephone company, the test of good communication is basically that of fidelity. If the message received is the same as the message sent, that is good; if it comes out distorted or incomplete, that is bad. It doesn't matter what you say, or why, or even how you say it. Say what you will; it's your nickel. This, then, marks a very different standard from that of either of the other two metaphors. And as such this model is applicable to all sorts of phenomena that can be treated as communication systems, with the potential result of regarding all phenomena as communication systems. Thus the human body is a communication system. For example, the central nervous system is a complex network of channels, sending messages to the brain as a kind of computer center; the brain reacts with immediate feedback or responses to what it has decoded. A family, a school, a town, a nation, or the globe and its stratospheric ecological extensions can all be regarded as separate and as related communication systems. In short, this simple model has possible applications far beyond that of interpersonal communication, which is not the case with either the dramatic or game models.

It is at this point that we should introduce some of Norbert Wiener's philosophy, for this notion of all aspects of life as communication systems or patterns of organization, as he identified them, is at the heart of his theory.

We start with that grim fact of the universe—entropy. The second law of thermodynamics state that in a closed system entropy tends to increase. From initial patterns of organization emerges disorganization, increasing randomness, and chaos. As William Butler Yeats put it in one of his most quoted poems, "Things fall apart. The center will not hold." Wiener himself waxes poetic on the theme: "shipwrecked on an island of organization in a sea of chaos."

The opposite of entropy is, of course, negative entropy, or organization. And what is it that will maintain organization? *Communication*. In a sense, all of Wiener's philosophy as expressed in *The Human Use of Human Beings* stems from this simple concept. A message, for example, is essentially characterized by its organization, its pattern. "Bob hit Bill" may be a message. If the order of words gets mixed up, it might come out "Bill hit Bob," which is still recognizeable as a message but not the right one. "Bill Bob hit" is further garbled, and if we imagine subsequent scramblings—Bil lBobh it—the message obviously becomes meaningless. But in a closed system, which we will explain shortly, this is exactly the tendency. Organization decreases and patterns become more random. For Wiener, people are also patterns of organization, and people eventually fall apart. Entropy is our nation's greatest killer! But Wiener is not at all pessimistic; indeed, he sometimes seems extraordinarily optimistic about the possibilities of human beings. Without going into details (nor does Wiener supply them), he speculates that just as a telegram can be sent from New York to Paris and interpreted as it was written in New York, it should also be possible to, as it were, "telegraph people," not the whole body, of course, but only patterns of information for the body. The human being is, for Wiener, only a complicated kind of message to communicate. If this sounds like science fiction, you should not be surprised to learn that Norbert Wiener, under the pen name of W. Norbert, wrote many science fiction books for amusement. But he is dead serious about the basic notion of organization.

We mentioned closed systems and implied the possibility of open systems. The difference is provided by feedback in a system. To use a simple example offered by Wiener, a thermostat attached to a furnace provides continuous feedback from the room to be heated to the furnace supplying the heat. When the room reaches the right temperature, the thermostat signals (communicates to) the furnace to turn off; when the room becomes too cool, another message is sent and the furnace heats up again.

If machines can perform such regulatory functions as controlling a furnace, or opening an elevator door only when it is in the proper position to be opened, then this frees humans to do more significant tasks; hence the title of Wiener's book. Since the publication of that book, computers have come to perform many regulatory functions, converting previously closed systems into open systems. In large cities all over the world traffic lights are computerized to adjust to the actual flow of traffic rather than just blink on and off in predetermined patterns. Major endeavors, such as space launches, would be impossible without the kind of cybernetic communication, the conversion of fixed closed systems into dynamic, responsive open systems.

But a technological advance, even one bolstered by a humane philosophy like Wiener's, does not necessarily guarantee any fundamental change in human behavior. Some housewives may now have mini-computers installed in their homes to do some of their routine work, but the machines can remain indifferent to the messages for attention and affection from their children. A nation's president can be computerized in some respects, but still fail to hear or heed the messages sent from the electorate and in that ignorance fail to respond to keep an open political system.

The concept of open or closed societies antedates the concept of cybernetics, and though less amazing and less amenable to applications in furnaces, elevators, or rockets, the principle is not very different. Without adequate feedback, without adjusting to the conditions that *are* rather than the conditions someone might want, things fall apart.

Moreover, the logic extended to social systems that fall apart fits well with cybernetics. The old tyrant, let us say, is unresponsive to the changes of the times and the demands of his people. The feedback, which might have come from his generals, messengers, or deputies, is lacking. Those who would tell him lack the courage, or perhaps those who did were punished, something that does not occur in the impersonal circuitry of computers. So along comes a new leader who is responsive to what is happening. He overthrows the tyrant and proclaims a new open society.

But a society means organization. Organization means hierarchy. Hierarchy often means that those most aware of what is occurring in society are the largest in number and the weakest in power. Their information must be fed back up through the system so that a much more limited number of people can in turn report to the new power at the center. If this communication is swift enough and accurate enough, and if the center of the organization responds appropriately to meet the demands and correct the problems, the system is viable. If not, then in time the system begins to close in upon itself, acting on what it thinks should happen, not what is happening. And then, things fall apart. The center will not hold. . . .

A Bit of Information

As if by some divine accident, the human nervous system and the computer nervous system have, apparently, at least one essential feature in common: both are based on a binary system, the simplest logic of on/off, yes/no, either/or.[28] Because the computer, inevitably, is simpler, let us begin there. Almost everybody in the United States or any industrialized part of the world is familiar with the computer card, even though most people probably have little idea how these cards are used. A card will have a certain number of slots punched into it, coded in accordance with some program, or purpose. When the cards are inserted into a computer prepared to read them, the computer will make electrical connections whenever there is a punch in the card. If there is no slot punched at a certain place, it makes no connection. Any information can be reduced to a combination or either/or choices. The alphabet used for English has twenty-six different characters. These can all be rendered into the binary system quite easily. Using 0 for no punch and 1 for a slot punched, we might punch out an alphabet card, like this: 01 = A; 11 = B, 10 = C; 101 = D; 110 = E; 111 = F; and so on.

The human nervous system, apparently, is similar in that a nerve cell, or synapse, either fires or it does not. It must reach a certain point or threshold before it fires, much like pulling on the trigger of a gun, but once that point is reached, it fires. And it is the succession of these firings that speed messages from a stubbed toe to the brain, which identifies the toe as the point of pain and instantaneously dispatches other messages, which result, in this case, in the body hopping around on the other foot. So like the computer, which appears to be complicated and varied in its reactions, if we trace the human electrical circuitry to its base we find it to be of the simple either/or logic.

Advancing binary logic a stage or two, we come to what is known as information theory. Essentially, much of this theory is an application of the either/or (yes/no) logic to complex units of information. Information theory is mostly in the province of communications, or the technological side of communication, but we can appropriate the theory for purposes of analyzing interpersonal communication as well. Indeed, we can do so with a simple game that is familiar to most people and made famous as a weekly radio program called "Twenty Questions." In this game one person thinks of something. He offers one of three broad categories—animal, vegetable, or mineral—as a clue. After that, the other players begin asking questions, and if they are

[28] The term *bit* as in "information bit" is an acronym made up of *bi*nary and di*git*.

skillful usually they can guess the correct answer within twenty questions. Each question must be phrased so that it is answered either with a yes or a no; no other kinds of answers are allowed. Thus the logic of the game is strictly binary, just like the nerve firings and the computer card punches. At first this might seem to be more a matter of luck. How could one guess, for example, "George Washington's axe handle" in fewer than twenty questions knowing only that it is classified as vegetable? Actually, it is not nearly as difficult as it seems, if one follows a strategy of successively narrowing the choices.

The first question should be one that will be general in order to eliminate a large number of possibilities. "Is it living?" is a pretty good first guess. A guess like, "is it that flower in the vase over there?" is a terrible first guess because the odds are that it isn't. And the answer leaves you more or less (one less, to be precise) where you were before. And so, as if moving up a pyramid of possibilities, the questions progressively narrow the choice until eventually it can only be one of two possibilities. This is the logic of deduction, the process of elimination, that Sherlock Holmes so often employed in discovering the culprit. Since it is based on either/or logic, it is ideally suited to computer use, and the computer can sort out and extrapolate conclusions much faster than the wise experts on the old "Twenty Questions" panel ever could.

What is meant by *information* in information theory is a measure of probability: the more probable, the less information; the less probable, the more information. Thus, in twenty questions the best or safest strategy is to ask questions of equal probability so that each time the possibilities are narrowed, the correct answer eventually seems probable. "Is it living?" offers equal probability of yes or no at the time it is asked. Told "no," the next question should again divide the probabilities equally, but because the field is narrower the total probability of a correct guess is increased.

Many interpersonal situations, conversations and our thinking about them, proceed in more or less the same way. Suppose a person is waiting at a bus station or airport with an hour or two to kill and he wants to talk to a stranger who is also waiting there. His first comment or question is likely to appear innocuous enough, even foolish: "Waiting for your plane?" or "Sure are a lot of people here," or something equally safe. The reply, however, will help to narrow the possible impressions of the other stranger—that he is friendly or not friendly, eager to talk to pass the time, too, or wants to be alone, and so on. In general, the successive remarks will reveal more and more up to some point at which questions seem to add no new information. At this point the person may not want to talk any more, or not want to talk about himself, and so on. One problem with trying to measure information on the basis of probability in social situations is that probability itself is difficult to ascertain, or perhaps we should say that probability is largely subjective, based on individual expectations and assumptions. Mr. A expected Mr. B to be friendly; but Mr. C expected Mr. B to be unfriendly. Moreover, friendliness of Mr. B is to a considerable extent a reaction to Mr. A or Mr. C.

A clearer measure of information would be in a public form, such as a newpaper headline. Setting aside for now the question of what makes news, generally the lower the probability that a certain event would occur, the greater the interest when it does occur. Banner headlines, like the exclamation point, are to be used for the big surprises. Those who would treat everything as amazing—like the letters of adolescent girls or ad writers—quickly destroy a normal patterning of probability and hence of information itself. If EVERYTHING is AMAZING, nothing is amazing.

Obviously, our treatment of information in newspaper headlines or even in conversation is not as simple as this. Long awaited news, even if it is expected, will still be afforded more attention—as if we were surprised—than the unexpected but less relevant news. And probably good news receives more attention, again in headlines or vocal inflections, than bad news. The computer model, so far as I can tell, does not accommodate itself to these factors. But imagine the headlines when it does!

It is also possible to distinguish kinds of interpersonal communication according to probabilities, redundancy, and information in the sense of information theory. As Wiener remarks, a cliché yields little information, a great poem a great deal of information. On a surface level of meaning, small talk is highly predictable, but, like those first questions in twenty questions, it is essential to lead the way to more detailed and less probable information. Conversations after funerals are highly predictable, as is nearly any form of communication associated with ritual, or repeated events. The purpose of our participation in such events is not to gain new information, but to celebrate a sense of continuity, and this necessarily means high predictability. In a church service the liturgy is usually ritualistic, highly probable, and one reason the faithful attend every Sunday; the sermon is about the only place where information can be put forth, and even most Sunday sermons are low on information and high on predictability. When the sermon is not predictable, when the minister challenges the congregation to act in ways in accordance to the credo, many may tune out his word seek another congregation. This, apparently, is a dilemma for many clergymen. Liberal sects, such as many reformed Jewish synagogues or Unitarians or radical Catholics, are likely to attract a large number of activists and people who participate in the congregation as an information and action center and not primarily for its ritual values. And talk of renaissance or revitalization of a congregation or indeed any institution is likely to mean a decrease in ritual forms and an increase in information. Then comes the question of how to strike a balance between both needs, for at every level, from perception to implementation, there is a limit to how much information can be taken in.

We should also note that many forums, ostensibly for presentation of information, may over a period of time decrease information and come to serve more ritual purposes. A number of studies of why people read the newspaper or watch TV news have confirmed this. Walter Cronkite is part of the evening ritual, and if he is on vacation, "it just doesn't seem the same," even if the same news is presented.

We can also relate probability and information to the concepts of perception and closure mentioned at the beginning of the book. We usually sense that we have correctly perceived or understood something when we can predict the result ahead of time. Suppose, for example, one takes a bus ride for the first time to visit a friend. He notices some landmarks along the way, where the bus turns, and so on. On his second trip he hopes he has taken the right bus. And he is reassured when he passes the landmarks he remembered and he also anticipates the upcoming landmarks. Another example could be listening to a lecture in class. At the beginning of the lecture the probabilities of knowing what the teacher will say are very low. Almost anything seems possible. As the student listens, if the lecture is a good lecture, the student will begin to nod, yes, that follows, which is to say "yes, I expected that sort of conclusion." If the lecture is too predictable with too little information, the student's nodding may be of another kind.

Animal, Vegetable, or Gzubszlkp

We have a problem with this approach. If I say, "animal, vegetable, or . . ." the probability is extremely high that the next word will be "mineral." These are words in a set expression, like "Tom, Dick, and you-know-who." And so "mineral" adds very little information; it was highly predictable. If instead of mineral I say "spiritual," that word conveys much more information, because it is not expected. But suppose we see printed, "animal, vegetable, or gzubszlkp." That last "word" should convey far more information, in terms of information theory, than even "spiritual," because it is a very unpredictable term. (If you noticed the preceding subheading, of course, it is somewhat more predictable to you.) Does this mean that the unexpected sneeze in a speech or typographical error in the newspaper conveys more information than any word that might fit in the slot? What of the works of the legendary monkeys typing in the British Museum, who could eventually produce the work of Shakespeare but who in all probability will produce some strange manuscripts in the process? Would their early drafts convey more information than even Shakespeare? The answer is (as expected) no. For to be a part of the potential information the words or symbols must be part of a finite code. These garbled words, or gibberish talk, and even sneezes, are outside of the code and, hence, in the category of noise. However, it is not always possible to identify, particularly in responding to another person who is talking or writing about something that one is unfamiliar with, what is information and what is noise in the channel. In the Bible, for example, there are places where the word *amen* (meaning roughly "right on") appears as if part of the original scripture. But Biblical scholars have discovered that some of these amens were actually scribbled into the margins of old manuscripts by eager monks. When the scriptures were copied (there being no printing presses at that time), a later scribe added this "noise" as part of the original message. A more pertinent, though less reliable, example is the appearance of the *th* sound in Castillian Spanish. Some *s* sounds are pronounced *th*—*cinco* sounding like *thinko*. Folk linguistics says a king lisped and his subjects, in obedience and to avoid embarrassment to the king, changed their pronunciation accordingly. The noise became part of the code itself.

In the early stages of interpersonal communication, then, part of what people are doing is attempting to perceive the nature of the code and to separate noise from the code. The person who begins a sentence: "like man, you know, man, I got wiped out on that test. Like I took gas, man, like . . ." reveals two kinds of information in those phrases. At first the words *man* and *like*, as this speaker uses them, help to identify him with a certain group, perhaps a certain life-style, and increases the possibilities of guessing many of his own values, interests, heroes, and the like. But soon thereafter, the appearance of *man* and *like* or certain vulgar expletives yield no information because they are so predictable.

A computer can only process information for which it is prepared. It does not adjust to the information being fed into it and filter out redundancies from the important information content. But people do, and do so in ways that vary from person to person. For one listener, "like man" in the speech of a person is a clue to identify with the person and listen more intently; for another, it is confusing, too much noise in the channel; for yet another, it serves to block out everything else that may be said.

Conclusion

Having presented briefly only three models (or metaphors) for viewing interpersonal communication, the reader may feel compelled to select one in the manner of multiple choice tests. If one is so inclined, then to be fair we must add the other two conventional options on such tests: none of the above and all of the above. Indeed, it may be that these last two are the most realistic. Clearly, every act of communication cannot be adequately described in the terms of any of these points of view. Perhaps nothing deadens one's sensitivity and curiosity more than an academic exercise, which renders vital, human interaction into encoder-decoder boxes, or presumes that the individuals must be performing for each other, or that they are inevitably competing in some perverse game. On the other hand, by considering at least these three perspectives, we may be led to ask questions we had not considered and to probe some underlying structure that could be helpful. Indeed, the value of such models or metaphors is not that they give us x-ray vision into any communication act, but that they give us different positions for viewing such acts. Moreover, because each participant in communication will define the situation differently, such alternative views of interpersonal communication may help us to see things as others might see them. It is quite possible that in a discussion one party is behaving in ways that suggest he sees himself as competing with another, using whatever resources he has to "score" in whatever manner he regards as significant. Another person, however, in that same situation may be viewing the process quite differently, and a third still differently.

Consider what transpires in some classrooms. There may be students who see the process as an elaborate competition—the essence of games—between themselves and the instructor, or the other students, or both. Payoffs may take different forms—grades, of course, but also approval, status, possibly a recommendation in the future. The instructor, noble fellow that he is in that noblest profession, may view his role differently; he dispenses information, facilitates discussion, and at least does his best to transmit his symbols with a minimum of distortion onto the notebook pages of his students. But there is also much to say about the classroom as a day time serial drama; teachers may be performers, too. And if our hypothetical teacher senses that some students see it all as a game, he may have to dramatize ways in which to show that it is not a game. The brightest of the game-playing students may have to play their parts in that drama, if only to score better at some later time.

There are some teachers who may define the classroom situation as a game. I have known a teacher—very effective, I was told—whose classroom presence was as an adversary of the students. He ridiculed students, he displayed an air of total self-confidence and utter contempt for his students, and he inspired great dislike. He taught logic. His students worked harder than most in order to find fault with his logic, in order to beat him at his own game. The outcome was often close to a classic game pattern. If the students won, then the teacher also won, for he had taught them something.

A basic distinction between viewing communication as a drama and viewing communication as a game is the element of conflict; conflict must be present in games but need not be present in a drama. If one grows up in a society that encourages competition and conflict, and particularly if one finds oneself in activities or a profession that is so characterized, it may be that the person carries this view of human relations into other spheres. The United States may be especially so characterized. And if that sounds negative, then the virtues of the game mentality are the fostering of values of equality (players must each have an equally fair chance from the beginning) and a lack of a begrudging spirit. When the game is over, one can start on the next game.

Other societies may encourage other views of human relations. In Japan, although there is much competition in some endeavors, there is also a strong reluctance to totally distinguish winners and losers, guilt or innocence. Even in a traffic accident all parties are a little bit innocent and a little bit guilty. In a society where hierarchies are clearly established and the code of conduct is a matter of great importance—in the military, in the priesthood, in bureaucracies, in communities of old, established families, and so on—the enactment of social dramas seems even more fitting than games. Thus while Goffman may apply his perspective to many situations in the United States, presumably there are some situations and some societies for which that view of interpersonal communication may be even more appropriate as defined by the participants, not merely as defined by Goffman or Burke or you.

This, then, may be the most important value of such models or metaphors: to interpret interpersonal communication not as it is, but as it might be defined by those participating in communication.

SEVEN
METHODS
OF ANALYSIS

Introduction

The study of communication is different from communication itself. Attempts can be made to examine this dynamic behavior by some appropriate means of analysis. To a considerable extent, of course, even as participants we are also analyzing communication. When we think, "I wonder what she meant by that," or ask ourselves, "now what's happening?" or suspect "this must be what he really wants to talk about," we analyze as participants and our very analysis influences the subsequent flow of communication.

In this book we have tried to emphasize a view of communication that could be held by participants, not merely by researchers in a laboratory or experimenters preparing conditions to test selected variables. There are risks in an analysis, no matter when or how it is performed. One risk is to give undue attention to some aspects, while ignoring others. When we are participating in communication, we may be biased by our own points of view, our own definitions of the situation, and our interpretations of the people in the conversation with us. We may be unduly optimistic, from our point of view, or unnecessarily suspicious. Even in listening to what is said, we may filter and distort what we hear and see. The dangers of subjective bias are well known, and perhaps few people—even trained specialists—are ever fully free from such distortions.

But there are also objective biases that we should watch out for. One of these is the risk of giving undue attention to that which is objectifiable—such as words recorded on a tape or facial expressions caught in a recording camera lens—while missing much that is significant simply because it was off camera or lacked an objectifiable category, such as an unfriendly mood, which we sense but cannot pin down. Naturally the further abstracted our record is from the real event, such as a typed script of a tape-recorded conversation, the more likely it is to lose nearly all of the paralinguistic elements of rate, pitch, and tone of voice, and even pause lengths, to say nothing of posture, facial expressions, and other nonverbal elements. Written transcripts are always simplifications.

A second bias is terminological and methodological. Studies of interpersonal communication are likely to give special emphasis to those aspects that have received attention through widely used terms (e.g., proxemics) and theories (e.g., dissonance). This suggests that two analyses of the same text, conducted at different times when different theories were in vogue, could receive different treatments and possibly different interpretations. This seems unavoidable by the very nature of analysis. Nevertheless we should be careful. Perhaps as a general principle, the student of communication would do well to learn about the theories and associated terms and then try to put these out of his mind when participating in or observing interpersonal communication in the hope that the earlier theoretical speculations will come back in a new, organic relationship, which more closely resembles the communication he is observing. To use another analogy from the drama, every line, every movement, and every bit of business contributes to the total effect of the drama, but the total effect is missed if in performance we try to be conscious of every line, every movement, and every bit of business.

Broadly speaking, there are two different but related subjects of analysis in interpersonal communication. One has been called content, surface meaning, and other names that refer primarily to the explicit stuff of the communication. Words, of course, but also facial expressions, gestures, and other bodily actions or movements, clothing, and so on are all included in this category. The other subject for analysis is called relationship factors, command functions, even meaning, and refers more to the implicit—why something is said and what the implications are for the other party. Cultural and group values, individual and collective definitions of the situation, and much more may be expected to be part of this category.

In this chapter we will briefly consider one approach to elucidating that second area through what has been called the attribution of meaning analysis. Then we will turn to a consideration of a dialectical approach and in the process try to relate some of the topics that have been introduced throughout the book thus far.

Attribution of Meaning

Foreign students in the United States—or Americans studying abroad—often come to a point where they speak and understand the language but still have problems in interpreting meaning at the interpersonal level. A foreign visitor meets a nice lady who says, "Stop by and chat any time you want"; he wonders if the lady was just trying to be friendly saying kind words, or if she really meant it. What advice should we give him? This problem of intention or communication patterning is not limited to persons from outside of one's culture, of course, but it is often in intercultural encounters that we become most aware of the fact that what words seem to say and how they are meant to be interpreted are often not the same, and that there is no direct parallel between them. The analogy to language study is obvious. We become most aware of the arbitrariness, special characteristics, and apparent illogic of our own language when studying another language. It is not surprising, then, that a very simple but useful method of analysis of interpersonal communication within a single culture was developed by scholars primarily concerned with intercultural communication.

Harry Triandis and his colleagues have offered a simple technique called the "attribution of meaning" to get at potential misunderstandings and conflicts in intercultural situations.[1] The same approach

[1] Harry Triandis, et al., *The Analysis of Subjective Culture* (New York: John Wiley, 1972).

serves equally well within our own culture. The method is so simple that, upon second thought, we recognize that it is not really very new at all. It seems very similar to a common technique in literary criticism and analysis for the oral interpretation of literature, in which the critic or reader constantly asks why this character said one thing or another and what his mood or intention was at the time. It is also similar to the technique of the actor who seeks some subtext, or underlying motivation, when rehearsing a particular line or action on the stage.

The procedure is to take a transcript of a short conversation and for every statement (or nonverbal equivalent) indicate what the speaker probably meant or intended by these words, and how the other person in the conversation is likely to have interpreted what was said. In conversations between people from different cultures, of course, we are more likely to find some variance in the two meanings attributed to a given statement based on differences in assumed role behaviors, definitions of the situation, cultural values, and so on. But even within the same culture, particularly if the persons participating in the communication are from different backgrounds and have different goals or values, similar misinterpretations can occur.

To illustrate the method, let us consider first an example provided by George Vassileu, a Greek psychiatrist, presented by Triandis.[2] These writers note that Greek employees often view supervisory roles as being more bossy than Americans do. The Americans tend to value and expect a more democratic or participatory procedure. Here then is what might occur when a Greek employee, expecting a bossy boss, interacts with an American employer, who expects a more symmetrical or participatory role for himself and his employee:

Behavior	*Attribution*
AMERICAN: How long will it take you to finish this report?	AMERICAN: I asked him to participate.
	GREEK: His behavior makes no sense. He is the boss. Why doesn't he tell me?

[2] Harry C. Triandis, "Culture Training, Cognitive Complexity and Interpersonal Attitudes," *Readings in Intercultural Communication*, Vol. III. (David Hoopes, ed.). (Pittsburgh: Regional Council for International Education, 1973), pp. 58–59.

Behavior	Attribution
GREEK: I do not know. How long should it take?	GREEK: I asked him for an order.
	AMERICAN: He refuses to take responsibility.
AMERICAN: You are in the best position to analyze time requirements.	AMERICAN: I press him to take responsibility for his own action:
	GREEK: What nonsense! I better give him an answer.
GREEK: Ten days.	AMERICAN: He lacks the ability to estimate time; this time estimate is totally inadequate.
AMERICAN: Take fifteen. Is it agreed you will do it in fifteen days?	AMERICAN: I offer a contract.
	GREEK: These are my orders: fifteen days.

In fact the report needed fifteen days of regular work. So the Greek worked day and night, but at the end of the fifteenth day, he still needed one more day's work.

AMERICAN: Where is the report?	AMERICAN: I am making sure he fulfills his contract.
	GREEK: He is asking for the report.
GREEK: It will be ready tomorrow.	Both attribute that it is not ready.
AMERICAN: But we had agreed it would be ready today.	AMERICAN: I must teach him to fullfill a contract.
	GREEK: The stupid, incompetent boss! Not only did he give me the wrong orders, but he does not even appreciate that I did a 30-day job in 16 days.
The Greek hands in his resignation. The American is surprised.	GREEK: I can't work for such a man.

This example illustrates the simple form of the attribution of meaning analysis. For every verbal expression (and, ideally, nonverbal expressions as well), meaning is attributed by the speaker and each of the listeners as noted. There are points where both attribute more or less the same meaning, points where their attributions diverge, and other points where at least one of the parties has no idea of what meaning to attribute. As mentioned before, when people share similar backgrounds, and experiences, and are familiar with each other, we should not expect to find so many differences of attributed meaning.

Keep in mind that (1) there is considerable guesswork involved in this approach—we cannot get into the heads of the people speaking to know what they may have meant—but also (2) in this analysis we are not trying to describe the darker side of a person's psychological state, or play psychiatrist in any way. Mostly, we are trying to make explicit what seems implied or assumed though not expressed directly. Perhaps it would be helpful, then to take a few other examples from everyday experience to show what kind of attributions might be made.

Two mothers of grade school children meet at a P.T.A. meeting for the first time.

Behavior	*Attribution*
MRS. LINCOLN: "Hello there, I'm Johnny Lincoln's mother.	MRS. LINCOLN: I'm being friendly and introducing myself to a mother of my son's classmate.
	MRS. WASHINGTON: She's friendly; she wants to start a conversation.
MRS. WASHINGTON: "Oh, you're Johnny's mother. Bobby always talks about Johnny.	MRS. WASHINGTON: I recognize the name and show I am friendly and have heard of her son.
	MRS. LINCOLN: She says she's heard of Johnny. She seems friendly— but I really wonder *what* her kid says about Johnny. I guess I am obliged to say I've heard of Bobby. I wonder, Bobby *Who?*
MRS. LINCOLN: "How nice. You must be Mrs.——	MRS. LINCOLN: I will be friendly and try to find out who she is.
	MRS. WASHINGTON: She seems friendly, but she doesn't seem to have heard of Bobby. She's asking me my name.
MRS. WASHINGTON: Washington. How do you do?	MRS. LINCOLN: She's giving her name. Now it's up to me to say something about her kid, I guess.

The basis for these attributions is, in this case, a projection from our similar experiences in such situations. There is no attempt here to read too much into the dialogue—particularly because this is a hypothetical example without any specific context apart from the P.T.A. meeting. Another person might make a somewhat different interpretation of the same words, of course, but we should expect a general agreement on what is transpiring here.

It may be helpful to look back at the brief analysis of the excerpt from *Love Story* presented in Chapter Three, for much of that was a kind of attribution analysis. Better still, you may want to find examples of your own in literature, even in comic strips, or recall recent conversations and examine those similarly.

The central characteristic and advantage of the attribution of meaning approach should be apparent. Meaning, from this point of view, is not in what is said or expressed nonverbally; rather, meanings are to be found in the others' interpretations of what is said or done. Although most sophisticated students of communication are aware that there is no built-in meaning in any word, gesture, or action, there may still be a desire by some to anchor meaning firmly to what is expressed and to the persons who do the expressing. Attribution of meaning, however, places the emphasis elsewhere. Although this view is very consistent with the perspectives of communication we have considered throughout this book, it also raises some very serious questions of responsibility, a matter that we will consider in more detail in the next chapter. We should deal with one such question at this point, however. If, in effect, meaning always depends more on how another person perceives and interprets what one says or does, what is the meaning of a concept like responsibility?

Suppose I say something that I intend as a compliment but is taken as an insult. Does that mean that only the attribution of an insult matters? For now we would like to say that it is not the only thing that matters, but that it matters perhaps more than what was intended. But note that if attribution of meaning shifts the responsibility to the perceiver or listener, it does not at all mean the acceptance of irresponsibility. Indeed it seems impossible for two persons to be irresponsible enough to hear whatever they wanted to hear and interpret whatever they wanted to interpret); if that were so, there could scarcely be any conversation at all. Moreover, if we recall the discussion of difficulties of marking beginnings and endings of communication, we will find that it is very difficult to place the full burden on any one person because everything that is said and done is in part a response to what has gone before. Thus, to reconsider the example mentioned previously of a person who interprets my compliment as an insult, we must consider that my desire to express a compliment at that particular moment and in that particular form was based on my attribution of the meanings of what preceded it.

Rather than pursuing this further into some form of infinite regress, let us turn instead to a more structured approach that may serve us well in the analysis of interpersonal communication.

The Dialectics of Dialogue

Some things come in twos, if not in actuality then at least in their symbolism: male and female, the sun and the moon, the Apollonian and the Dionysian, life and death. Dialectical reasoning finds little support among scientists and generally has never been very fashionable in the United States. Still, as a method of reasoning and analysis, the dialectical method is among the oldest and most widely spread—from the Socratic questions that served as major educational philosophy to the question-answer catechism of the Roman Catholic Church. In Hegelian dialectics, later appropriated, expanded, and expounded by Marx, there are essential antagonistic forces in the world whose relationship proceeds from thesis and antithesis, which results in a synthesis; this in turn becomes the next thesis. The laws of opposing forces in Oriental thought—the *yin* and *yang* of Taoism—are similar in form if not in function. As we noted earlier, the logic of the computer is a binary logic of an either/or sort, and to that extent it resembles the logic of the firing of nerve connections in the human body.

It may be, too, that some aspects of interpersonal communication can be described and analyzed by a dialectical system. Already we have introduced several dual concepts that might form the basis for such a system. In this section we will briefly review these, add additional pairs of terms, and suggest applications for analysis of a variety of forms of verbal interaction among people.

One of the most widely known and used of the dialectical patterns is that developed by Robert F. Bales many years ago on the basis of small group discussion transcripts.[3] Bales organized the kinds of remarks made in most discussions into six pairs, usually presented in the form of the chart that follows. Although the Bales chart is not usually identified as a dialectical system, it is clearly that. Some are questions and answers, some are generally positive or negative (e.g., gives support, withholds support, and so on as shown in the diagram. Because these categories are abstracted but still sufficiently clear and distinguishable, they may be applied to the analysis of not only small group discussions, but also to conversations between two persons, and to the

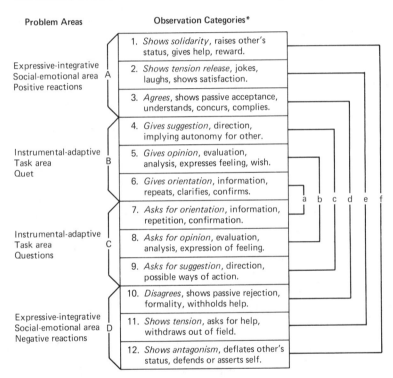

*A subclassification of system problems to which each pair of categories is most relevant:

    a. Problems of orientation.   d. Problems of decision.
    b. Problems of evaluation.   e. Problems of tension-management.
    c. Problems of control.   f. Problems of integration

[3] Robert F. Bales, *Interaction Process Analysis* (Cambridge: Addison-Wesley, 1953).

interior monologue of the stream of consciousness, or to those rare occasions when one talks to oneself aloud—such as when packing a suitcase ("Let's see, do I have my toothbrush? Yes, I have my toothbrush. Why am I taking this?").

Bales and many others who have scrutinized small group discussions distinguish between task-oriented remarks and socio-emotional remarks. For those who expect symmetry if not elegance in communication, their finding that groups tend to require a balance between both should be heartening, if not surprising. All work and no play make Jack's group a dull group; or, better said, it is very difficult to have a group that is characterized only by one or the other. The coffee break may be the institutionalized form of a more general need—to relax, release tensions, or break from the routine task.

Yet another pair of concepts to come out of small group studies, and closely related to the themes that we will discuss next, is that of process, or procedure and content. This deserves somewhat more attention. In order for any group or any sort of organization or system to operate, certain rules or procedures must exist. Will there be a leader, or should leadership be shared? Should there be an agenda or not? Should we put things to a vote or should we encourage consensus? And so on. The number of possible procedural questions is enormous; the number of necessary decisions is less formidable. Nevertheless, when a group or organization begins to form, before any real discussion can take place, some things must be generally understood.

Many of the studies of group behavior have been based on so-called T-groups (training groups), in which people come together primarily to study themselves as a group. "You are free to do as you like," the trainer may tell them. The delight of such total freedom, however, may soon give way to competing preferences in how to proceed. With no requirements and no identified leader, the group seeks to assert, invent, or impose upon itself at least a minimal structure. In real life, of course, most of us enter organizations or institutions—whether the family, or the university, or our society—in which the basic rules are already established, though most of them are not explicit. What seems particularly interesting in the findings of the small group researchers is the frustration one feels when having to help formulate rules. Even within, or perhaps especially within, the freedom of the T-group, there is a great desire to get on with the discussion and to get the procedural matters done with quickly. And yet, it is extremely difficult—as you may know if you have participated in such a group—to reach a quick, common agreement about procedures. Thus the tension of the dialectic: before moving to content, the procedure must be established; and any procedure, obviously, will influence the content. This, of course, is precisely the dynamic of the T-group, at least in its early stages, for the arguing about the procedure in turn becomes the content for later review and analysis. Some groups never get beyond that.

The American democratic system, many have said, is primarily a system of procedure, of process. The First Amendment guarantees certain rights of freedom of speech, freedom to assemble, and so on. It does not say anything about the content of the speech or about purposes of assembling. Thus it is not surprising that many courses and books on discussion or group process have stressed the values of democratic decision-making and of the democratic system. At the same time many who have expressed fears of group dynamics, often using the Orwellian pejorative "group think," have tended to support more conservative social and political positions.

In sum, one dialectical theme is that of procedure and substance, or process and content. These are interdependent, but conversations and discussions can be interpreted as shifting from one aspect to the other or of being focused so much on one that the other is frustrated. The uneasiness that a stranger sometimes feels in the midst of a group of old friends may be interpreted in this way, too. The new member must pay attention to the implicit procedural norms as well as the content of the discussion, whereas the others need to give little attention to the former.

Interpersonal Relationships: Symmetrical and Complementary

Although there are many possible descriptions of kinds of interpersonal relationships, let us return to the simple distinction that was introduced earlier, that of symmetrical and complementary relationships. For convenience we will consider these as distinct; in application, however, the distinction may be more of degree rather than clear-cut separation. A symmetrical relationship is primarily based on the assumption of equal or identical roles, rights, statuses, and the minimizing of any apparent differences, such as that of age or sex. In short, in a symmetrical relationship, what one person does or says, the other person could also do or say. Culturally, as we noted earlier, the United States has stressed values that encourage symmetrical relationships in marriage, in the family, in organizations of many kinds. Complementary relationships, on the other hand, are characterized by valuing and emphasizing differences between people. Thus the existence of a symmetrical relationship may be said to have come about despite a person's being older or younger, male or female, and so on. In a complementary relationship we might say the feeling should be because a person is older or younger, male or female, he or she is valued. Thus the relationship between an identified leader and follower, a boss and his or her employee, the mother and her infant, and so on are complementary.

Of course it is not always wise or even easy to make clear-cut distinctions, but the broad differences in a particular setting are frequently implicit in who speaks first, what one says, where each person stands or sits, who asks permission and who gives permission, and so on. Almost any definition of a communication situation will reflect either a more complementary or more symmetrical relationship, and the ensuing conversation will also be influenced by the defining characteristics of these two alternatives. And if, as sometimes happens, one person expects a symmetrical relationship and the other expects a complementary relationship, certain complications can be anticipated.

Content and Relationship

A second pair of terms for a dialectical theory of communication are those of the content—the surface *meaning* of what is said, and the *relationship*, or its implications for the interpersonal relationship in which the expression occurs. Sometimes what seems to be smooth communication at the surface or content level implies abrupt changes in the relationship of the parties who are communicating. And conversely, sometimes an uneven surface content of remarks exchanged actually has little influence on the relationship of the people speaking. Obviously, the relationship aspect of this pair is closely related to the previous distinction between symmetrical and complementary relationships.

Before continuing, it may be helpful to illustrate these two pairs of concepts. Consider the case of a high school boy who visits a medical doctor. After waiting for some time in the outer office, the receptionist tells the boy, "the doctor will see you now." The boy enters. "May I close the door?" he asks the doctor. "Of course," the doctor replies. "Please be seated." The boy sits and stares at the floor. "What seems to be the problem?" the doctor asks. "It's . . . it's not about me, you know, it's about a friend. He has this problem, see. . . ."

A student making a simple analysis, using the concepts of symmetrical-complementary and content-relationship, might come up with these observations. The situation is defined both by the boy and the doctor as a complementary relationship; the doctor's role is quite different from the role of the boy or of any patient. This is, surely, common knowledge, about doctor-patient relationships, but we can also confirm this through such evidence as (1) the boy had to wait for permission to enter the office; (2) he asked the doctor if he could close the door; and (3) we can assume that the doctor might be wearing a white gown or be seated behind a desk, or we can imagine various nonverbal factors in the setting that add to his dramatization of the role of the doctor as different from that of the patient.

The boy asked if he could close the door (content), which may signify more than a simple question of how to act, having opened the door. It might mean, to the doctor, that the boy has a rather confidential problem as opposed to, for example, asking some questions about entering medical school. It may also mean that the boy hopes to establish a more personal relationship with the doctor, one of trust that must not be threatened by other patients outside or even by the nurse. The boy stares at the floor, which again may be interpreted in various ways, but at least one interpretation might be a special nervousness in not expressing his reason for coming to the office right away.

And then the boy says that the problem is not his problem but that of a friend. It is well known that many people with certain problems, particularly those that they feel embarrassed or ashamed about, may talk about their problem as if it were somebody else's problem. And it is likely that the doctor will at least consider this as a possible real meaning, which in turn has implications for his relationship with the boy. That is, if the boy can feel he can fully trust and confide in the doctor, everything will go much more smoothly; and so it is now up to the doctor to respond in such a way that alters their relationship to reduce the ambiguity if nothing else. The doctor might choose to be very direct: "See here, young man, if your friend has a problem he should come in; if it is really your problem, just say so. I'm sure no matter what your problem is it is not the first time I've faced it, and if you are frank with me I can help you." Or the doctor might be more cautious, less directive: "About your friend, is it? You want to help your friend?" And so on. In any case, these responses of the doctor will be directed to alter and redefine more precisely that particular situation.

1. *Response to Content, Response to Relationship.* In a conversation we are not simply saying words and reacting with other words; we are also sensitive to the unstated meanings or possible meanings of words. Whether we choose to respond to words or to what might have been intended by the words is thus another dual choice. In recent years there has been an effort to encourage people to listen for hidden meanings, or implications by writers and teachers in such fields as counseling, sensitivity training, nonverbal awareness, and the like. And so it may be, though I have no way of knowing, that we hear more explicit references to relationships, or implied meanings today than we would have heard fifteen or even five years ago. That is, some parents may often say to children something like, "You say you will do it, but I think you mean you are angry that I asked you to do it." Some college students may say to each other, "Don't give me that 'it's very interesting' crap—tell me what you feel!" Certainly in many sensitivity training or encounter groups, this sort of expression of current feelings is emphasized. A simple surface exchange is regarded as a cop-out. At any rate, this distinction can be noted at specific points in a conversation, as characteristic of a particular person in a conversation, or even as a norm for the conversation. If this is the norm, it may appear to be a very peculiar conversation from without.

To illustrate this, consider two sets of examples, the first with a response at the surface verbal level, the second with a response to the covert relationship level:

1. "Do you mind if I interrupt you for a minute?"
   "No, I don't mind."
   "You sure?"
   "Yeah, I'm not busy. What do you want?"
2. "Do you mind if I interrupt you for a minute?"
   "No, I don't mind."
   "Well, you're being polite. I think you do probably mind."
   "No, I'm not busy, what do you want?"
   "Oh, come on—I can see you are busy. But since I have already interrupted you . . . "

In both examples, one person replies, "No, I don't mind." This could be said in many ways to convey a genuine feeling that the speaker doesn't mind or to make it clear that he probably does mind but feels obliged to say that he doesn't. The more sincere the words seem to the other person—that is, the more they can be taken at face value—the less likely he may be to openly doubt those words as in the second example. However, even if one person is quite sure that the other person does mind, the conversation changes dramatically if he actually expresses that doubt. One might say there is a shift from the focus on the content to a focus, if only momentarily, on the relationship level. This leads to a more complicated kind of dialogue. Indeed, in an extreme, this sort of shift lends itself to parody, satire, and social commentary of the kind that is deftly presented by Jules Feiffer in many of his cartoons, often by Charles Schulz in his "Peanuts" strip, and by the old sophisticated routines of Mike Nichols and Elaine May in their brutally funny dialogues. (These artists were well in advance of the academics who later pursued these issues in the classroom.)

To put this another way, the first exchange can be seen as a highly predictable one of informal but polite questions and responses. The effect is to begin and conclude with the questioner being subordinate (because he is asking the favor) to the one he has interrupted. In the second case, however, the exchange is not only much less predictable and mechanical, and rather less polite, but it also tests the relationship between the two. For the would-be subordinate becomes a kind of accuser (doubting the other's sincerity). Later in this book we will return to this kind of exchange, for it raises some interesting questions about ethics and awareness in communication. (If the person who said, "No, I don't mind," expressed this in a way that really seemed to indicate that he did mind, he places the visitor in a difficult situation.)

A friend in the army tells of a related exchange. The wife of a lower-ranking officer telephoned the wife of a superior officer to invite them over for dinner. The conversation went something like this:

"Mrs. Blake, we were wondering if you and Captain Blake could come to our home for dinner this Thursday evening?"

"Thank you very much, Mrs. Smith. That's very nice of you. Unfortunately, Tom and I have another engagement that evening."

"Oh, that's too bad. Well, perhaps on Friday, then."

"Friday . . . Oh, I'm terribly sorry, but we are having friends over that evening. I am sorry."

"Would Saturday or Sunday be possible?"

"Gee, it's funny, but I'll just have to beg off this weekend—in fact, we are gone almost every weekend. But thank you for asking us, anyway."

"Well, then, how about Monday or Tuesday of next week?"

"Mondays we have our bowling, and Tuesdays we like to be home with the children. You know how it is. Some other time, perhaps. Thank you, anyway."

"Mmm, I see. What about next Wednesday?"

"Oh hell, let's get it over with. What time this Thursday do you want us to come?"

One way of looking at this conversation is that it is a series of only two basic messages: (1) "We want you to come to dinner," and (2) "We don't want to come." This seems clearest, of course, in the final blunt reaction of the captain's wife. And some people, who have heard this dialogue, blame that wife for being so blunt. Others, however, criticize the other wife for not catching on sooner, and some have even praised the captain's wife for telling it like it is. But in any case, the relationship between these wives is now clearer, though one can wonder about what kind of evening the two couples will spend on Thursday. Clarifying relationships through more explicit content does not necessarily make for more enjoyable communication.

2. *Identification and Disassociation.*   In word choice, paralanguage, and nonverbal behavior, a person's response to another may serve to reinforce or express some kind of identification with that person (or his or her remarks). Or, a response may express disassociation. One person may greet another saying, "Hi. Sure is a nice day." The person so greeted may be obliged to respond somehow, but if he says "Sure is," in the same tone of voice as the person who greeted him or if he says, "What's so good about it?" he expresses an obvious difference in relationship. Certainly it is not a simple matter of choice of words. Even "What's so good about it?" can be said in a playful, friendly-sarcastic way, which does not necessarily show antagonism. So we must pay attention to how things are said, and not just reckon with words alone. This in turn anticipates complications of interpretations—the outside observer interprets as unfriendly something that the people conversing did not so interpret, or one person interprets it that way, the other interprets it differently, and so on. But as a category for analysis, something like identification or the opposite is useful.

3. *Verbal Interaction.*   The "logic" of conversations or other forms of interpersonal communication also proceed in sequences of twos. These procedural forms function to give direction to a discussion, to guide each party in what to say or not to say, and to help "punctuate" the flow of communication. Often when a pair is incomplete or seems to be overly complete with conflicting responses, the communication goes awry. Let us consider a few of the most common patterns:

A. *Questions and Answers:*   One of the most common "logics" in conversation is that of questions and answers. Greetings frequently follow a question-answer pattern. And nearly as frequently the answer itself contains another (or the same) question: "How are you?" leads to "Fine, thanks. How are you?" Speeches, opening remarks at meetings, bull sessions, or rap sessions, are all likely to begin with questions of some sort: "Shall we begin?" "Now what should we do?" "You ready to go?" They function much like the greeting pattern, requiring a response that usually is highly predictable and in surface content rather uninformative.

Within a longer conversation, a question is often used to alter the direction of the discussion. If at some point in a discussion you wonder aloud, "How did we ever get talking about this?" you may find, if you trace the conversation back, that it was a single question or a series of questions and answers that moved the discussion to some initially unplanned-for topic. Thus a second function of questions and answers is to mark shifts or phases in conversations, and as such these serve as significant means of punctuation.

Yet another function is simply to keep a conversation going. Again, because a question demands an acknowledgment if not a plausible answer, we frequently ask questions because we know that at least there must be some response to keep the talking going. If you were to listen to conversations that sound like the two people are not really very interested in each other or the subject of the conversation but must keep talking out of politeness or to ward off the anxiety of silence, you will find that many of these are characterized by a regular, if listless, question and answer pattern. Often in these cases there is some social pressure to balance the number of questions asked by each party, which in turn can add to the awkward sense of talking to avoid silence; thus a typical conversation of two housewives who do not know each other in some waiting room:

"Do you come here often?"
"Me? Hmm, yes. Sometimes."
"Oh. That's interesting."
"Do you?"
"Come here? Often? Not so often."
Silence.
"Do you live near here?"
"Yes, not too far. . . . How about you?"
"Very close."
"That's convenient, isn't it."
"Yes. What about you?"

Whether the relationship is symmetrical or complementary will influence the role of questioner and answerer. In symmetrical relationships there need be no expected order of who questions whom, unless one of the parties has special information or experiences to share with others. A close friend who returns from a fascinating trip may do much more answering than asking, or if a conversation turns to a subject about which one is especially knowledgeable, he or she may receive many questions. But even in some of these cases, if the relationship is truly symmetrical, the person being asked questions may feel uncomfortable after a time and may make some attempt to ask others questions to bring their roles into balance.

B. *Assertion and Responses:* Assertions are often disguised questions or questions with implied answers. In any case, they demand some response even if the response is only an acknowledgment of having heard the assertion. In small talk, assertions like "Looks like rain," "Nice talking to you," "You're looking great," elicit acknowledgments such as "Sure does," or "Right," or simply "Thanks—you, too." Acknowledgments may be unexpressed verbally—the nod of a head, a smile, or a wave. But some response is normally expected; indeed, there are times when if no response is given, the person who made the assertion may switch to a question ("Did you hear me?"), or may even repeat with more emphasis the original assertion ("I said, 'nice day'!").

Generally it seems that the longer the assertion and the more fully it is embedded in a conversation, the less the need or possibility of responding to it. And also, the more general the assertion and the more generally directed (if there are several in a conversation), the less need there is for a clear response from any one individual.

C. *Initiation and Closure:* It sometimes happens in conversations that one person begins a sentence, and at some slight pause the other person completes the sentence. Often this is to demonstrate or test the listener's understanding of the speaker's intention. Thus, from the Nixon tapes:

PRESIDENT: Your view is that what will happen on it, that it's going to come out. That something is going to break loose, and—
DEAN: Something is going to break and—
PRESIDENT: It will look like the President—
DEAN: Is covering up—
PRESIDENT: Has covered up a huge (unintelligeible)
DEAN: That's correct.[4]

[4] *The Presidential Transcripts* (with commentary by the staff of *The Washington Post*) (New York: Dell Publishing Co., 1974), p. 137.

Identifying who initiates and who provides the closure and how this exchange functions (self-assertion of the one providing the closure, a kind of stooge role as in comedy acts, which are found all over the world; as a sign of respect and attentiveness; as prompting or assisting the person who starts the sentence, and so on) can be very revealing in analyzing conversations or simply better understanding one's own communication habits. It appears that this pattern may more often occur as friendship increases or when a certain eagerness or excitement is generated—as if the person completing the sentence cannot wait to hear the speaker finish but must finish it himself. At any rate, this is yet another two-part pattern of conversations.

We can advance this general principle to include, not only the sentence, but possibly a paragraph or a segment like the first part of an explanation. The person responding to this might say something like: "Let's carry this another stage, because I think I see what you are getting at," then he continues for several sentences adding to the original idea. Sometimes more formal group presentations proceed this way: "John will explain the background, and I will present the current situation."

D. *Statement and Restatement:* As we mentioned in introducing the theory and methods of counseling identified with Carl Rogers, acknowledging a comment by restating the comment is another pattern. There is a certain degree of ambiguity in this form of response. At a minimum it reveals that a comment made previously was heard; to a slightly greater extent it implies that the comment heard was understood; beyond this is the possibility that the remark was not only heard and understood but also accepted—at least no overt objection was expressed. On the other hand, it offers no overt evidence of agreement or support, and thus is a kind of oral Rorschach in which the original speaker can perceive agreement or lack of agreement as he chooses.

Although the positive nature of such remarks has been amply described in Rogerian literature, we must also recognize that the very suspicious or defensive speaker can distrust or be made to feel uncomfortable by a respondent who consistently says "Hmm mmm," and then restates more or less what was said. Rogers himself, of course, has stressed the need for the right atmosphere in which acceptance and trust can be fostered, and thus the technique of restatement must be seen in the content of that supportive atmosphere. Take the same technique and put it in the hands of a severe judge or police officer, whose setting is more likely to produce feelings of self-consciousness and anxiety, and we can readily imagine the uncertainty about the meanings of restatements.

E. *Information and Cliché:* Closely related to the two previous patterns is the distinction in information based on probability. Although the measurement of the amount of information on the basis of probability is a matter of degree rather than an either/or distinction, we may temporarily propose two broad alternatives: one we can call information, meaning here that the comment was not readily predictable on the basis of the previous flow of conversation or knowable from the past comments of the individual; and the other we can call cliché, which means that there is relatively little that surprises us in the comment—either anyone is likely to have said that at that time, or one particular person was likely to say such and such because that person always seems to use a particular expression, or turn to a particular topic or theme under similar conditions.

The distinction between symbols and signs, emphasized by those in the general semantics school, is a parallel distinction.[5] When a word elicits many possible reactions depending on its context, who says it and where, the word functions as a symbol. When, however, a word consistently elicits one reaction (for a particular person or for many people), it functions as a sign, the reaction popularly known as a signal reaction. Thus some so-called emotion-charged words, which for some people produce anger, or blushing, or fear, or pride, and so on, seem to elicit signal reactions. This means that signal reactions are highly predictable and are similar in some ways to what we are calling clichés. Symbolic reactions, on the other hand, are more difficult to predict and are more in the area of information.

Probably we all know people who get turned on or turned off by certain words or names of people. And we may feel that we can easily guess what their reactions will be when such and such a subject comes up in a conversation. "We've heard it all before," we might think, or "here we go again." Naturally when we are surprised to find the person reacts quite differently for a change, being calm instead of excited,

[5] See John Condon, *Semantics and Communication,* 2nd ed. (New York: Macmillan, 1975), pp. 7–11.

saying something pleasant instead of critical, or vice versa, what had been cliché becomes extraordinarily significant. Outside of the field of interpersonal communication is the analysis of foreign propaganda. Analysts will watch for the slightest change in wording, the mention of something not mentioned before, or the failure to mention something that was mentioned before. To one not aware of the expectations, this concern seems excessive, but to those who study reports, speeches, and news dispatches daily, total shifts in foreign policy can be hinted at simply by the mention or absence of a particular word or phrase.

Conclusion

In this chapter we have tried to relate a number of concepts presented earlier. The notion of attribution of meaning reminds us of the interdependence of persons who participate in communication or, if you prefer, the transactional view of interpersonal communication. I speak, but the meaning is largely yours. And by the same token, what I say or how I act will depend on my interpretations of your previous remarks and behavior.

To provide some structure for examining many forms of interpersonal communication, particularly those that include verbalization, we considered a series of dialectical relationships. A dialectical system may be merely a fancier name for an imposed system of dualities, of course, and we mustn't make more of this view than of any of the other models or metaphors considered earlier. And yet the defining characteristic of such dialectics does seem to fit well with all three of the models we have mentioned: the performer and his audience, the players in competition, and even the dualities of the cybernetic model—the binary logic, the data and the instructions on how to treat the data (the program), and so on. Perhaps if we are seeking some unification among the different perspectives it can be found in—or created by—interdependent dualities.

One other possible advantage of this view as a means toward some unifying theory is that it may fit well with other well-known interpretations of communication that are not included in this book, such as the

---

[6] Leon Festinger, A *Theory of Cognitive Dissonance* (Evanston: Row, Peterson, 1957).

theory of cognitive dissonance advanced by Leon Festinger,[6] or the balance theory of Fritz Heider.[7] Although we will not discuss these here, they are mentioned in passing because they, too, are based on a binary logic (dissonance and consonance; balance and imbalance). Such theories have been helpful in predicting what kinds of communication will occur with what effects under certain circumstances, and in offering at least partial explanations. Students in interpersonal communication courses in which these theories are presented may consider these in relationship to what we have discussed. Perhaps all of these theories will someday be conjoined under a broader and in some ways older theory of stasis, which views interpersonal communication as essentially seeking some steady state of total predictability. But that begins to sound like physics, and archaic physics at that, so let us leave such speculations and turn to the uniquely human concerns of the ethics of interpersonal communication.

[7] Fritz Heider, *The Psychology of Interpersonal Relations* (New York: John Wiley and Sons, 1958).

EIGHT
ETHICS: RESPONSIBILITY IN COMMUNICATING

There is surprisingly little talk—or writing—about the ethics of inter-personal communication. Those who regard the study of communication as primarily a social science tend to view their task as describing what people do, not what they should do. They may say that we must first understand what *is* before asking what *ought* to be.

Certainly that is a reasonable position, or at least one we have come to feel comfortable with. When a scientist makes the move from the *is* to the *ought*, he discards his role as a scientist. There are other reasons, more generally shared, for avoiding discussions of ethics in communication. Even the word *ethics* sounds old-fashioned, and maybe too pious, even pretentious. Who has the right to judge what is right? It has taken centuries to rid ourselves of some narrow-minded notions of right and wrong, and we must not now lose what has been gained by returning to some new puritanism. The social sciences, probably most of all, have increased our understanding and respect for people who act differently, and merely labeling an action as wrong inevitably gets in the way of understanding.

Moreover, the world seems to have changed so rapidly that this is a very poor time to suggest standards of ethical behavior that would apply broadly across a generation, let alone an entire culture. What was good for our parents may not be good for us; and what may be good for us may not be good for our neighbors. Thus recently we have come to speak of situational ethics, relative to specific individuals in specific situations.

And yet, just as a culture is given some shape through patterns of values, an individual's sense of self and his or her relationship with others is given shape at least partly through some pattern of ethical choices. In most cases, it has seemed to me, choices related to the issues of interpersonal communication, which we have been considering, do not stem from any explicit ethical code. Even teachers of communication, who may have fairly strict ethical standards about academic work (don't cheat, don't plagiarize, even don't brownnose, and so on) are not likely to offer ethical advice about daily encounters in interpersonal communication. One finds more guidance from Ann Landers than from most writers in the communication field.

When scholarly research methods are criticized, as in some experimental studies that require deception, or when there are findings that might threaten valued forms of communication, as with fears of brainwashing techniques or subliminal persuasion, then the issue of ethics emerges. And when individuals or institutions in the public trust—the president or the FBI or the CIA, for example—are publicly criticized for overstepping their rights, then again the ethical issue emerges. Probably the one area in speech communication that constantly involves ethical issues is freedom of speech. Law and particularly constitutional rights provide standards for what may and may not be said, done or not done. We might also note in passing that some of the modern great scientists, whose work is centrally related to interpersonal communication, have tended to speak out on ethical issues. Norbert Wiener, B. F. Skinner, Carl Rogers, and Noam Chomsky are four contemporary thinkers who have written from very different positions, but all have consciously tried to go from the *is* to the *ought*. But that is always something of a leap, even for the academic giants who are accustomed to taking giant steps.

It also seems surprising, to me at least, that religious writings have offered relatively little guidance in the ethics of interpersonal communication. None of the Ten Commandments says "Thou shalt not lie"; perhaps the closest we come is the injunction not to bear false witness against another, which presumably condemns gossip, innuendo, and perjury. But what of publicly praising someone you do not like, or exaggerating claims for yourself? In what might be the Confucian version of the Ten Commandments there is the urging not to talk too much. While those of us from the West might appreciate this advice, we have no comparable tenet in scripture or classical aphorism.

Nearly every concept, principle, or theme mentioned in this book can be interpreted in terms of better or worse, desirable or undesirable, ethical and unethical. As rather abstract ideas, they may help to describe what is; in practice they imply consequences that cannot be separated from what one feels ought to be. These ethical issues are by no means clear-cut or easily dealt with. Each ethical theme we will mention can, at some point, clash with an alternative theme. And at that point we may be forced to act on one or the other. Should you speak your mind, be true to yourself, if it may mean upsetting another person? What if your personal conscience conflicts with the role you have been selected to perform; where does your greater loyalty lie? If you have been entrusted to keep a secret, but, having heard the secret, you feel it should be brought out into the open, what will you choose? In your mind, what distinguishes an innocent lie from an outrageous fabrication? Let us consider some of these familiar ethical issues in our daily communication behavior.

Candor

For want of a better word, let us consider candor as one possible ethical principle of interpersonal communication. *Honesty* might be substituted, but that word seems more ambiguous about the standard of truth. *Honesty* suggests, to me at least, a greater measure of objectivity, whereas *candor* suggests a more subjective or personal expression like "calling them as I see them," or being frank, and otherwise not disguising what one personally believes or feels.

We are likely to have strong feelings about the virtue of candor; culturally our slogans have varied from time to time—"plain speaking," "telling it like it is," "letting it all hang out," and so on, but Americans particularly have praised those who speak out. We have little respect for people who seem to hedge, or who speak out of two sides of their mouths, or even who speak in generalities.

The kind of candor that Americans seem to value cannot be easily separated from the value of equality and individuality, and symmetrical interpersonal relationships. As we have also noted, it is not easy for a person in a subordinate position to speak as bluntly to his or her boss or superior as it is for the superior to speak bluntly to the subordinate. "Yes, sir," and "yes, ma'am," are often the expressions—literally—of inferiority. As such the "yes" is more likely to mean "I understand," or simply "whatever you say—you are the boss," rather than agreement. But we would like *no* to mean *no;* we would like a person who does not understand to say so, and a person who disagrees to express that disagreement directly. "Correct me if I am wrong." "Let's get this out in the open." "Speak up if you have any questions." "Let me know what you think." These expressions are heard in families, in schools from kindergarten through college, in business, and in nearly any organization that would espouse a democratic spirit, a spirit that demands symmetrical relationships among members, even if some have positions of leadership.

If candor, equality, and individualism go together, then perhaps by increasing the settings and atmosphere for candor, equality and individualism are also increased. Conversely, if we establish institutions, whether they be classrooms or marriages, where one party is not really free to say what he or she really thinks, then we threaten both the values of equality and individualism. To some extent the power or liberation movements of the 1960s and 1970s in the United States (black power, red power, brown power, women's lib, and so on) were demands for individualism and equality, and these demands came through most clearly by urging candor. Blacks shared with other blacks things that had been withheld, and then told whitey for once what they really felt. Women shared with other women things that had been withheld because women weren't supposed to think like that or talk that way, and then let the male establishment know what women really thought. What is interesting is that the sudden candor went a long way in achieving some of the espoused goals of equality and acceptance as individuals—e.g., to be treated as a unique person, not a Negro, and not a woman or a wife.

In summary, we could say that one ethical principle of interpersonal communication is not to discourage, in any way, candid expressions of feelings. There must be no threats or punishments for speaking out, no ostracism, not even any subtle symbolic listening. Put positively, we must do what we can to encourage openness, trust, and genuine sharing of honest beliefs and feelings.

But . . . read on.

Social Harmony

Although the ethics of frank expression of feelings may facilitate symmetrical relationships of individuals, they may sometimes run into conflict with another value, that of social harmony. Probably everyone at one time or another avoids saying what he or she really believes in order to avoid hurting somebody's feelings, giving offense, or creating a scene. We lie, if that is what it is to be called, we say nothing, we equivocate, we change the subject. Moreover, we may find a person who always speaks bluntly to be obnoxious or at least too self-centered. And while these examples suggest that we tend to avoid saying unpleasant things, we also sometimes avoid saying pleasant things for fear of how they might be taken. Most people do not walk up to a stranger and say "you're beautiful," or "you're handsome," or "I'd love to go to bed with you," even if they might be thinking such thoughts. Whether or not our society would be better if we did so is another issue.

Where interdependence is valued over individualism, where complementary relationships (stressing and valuing differences) are valued over symmetrical relationships (which stress and value similarities or likenesses), we may find that keeping social relationships harmonious is more valued than speaking out our minds. Japan provides an excellent model of a culture with these values, just as the United States provides an excellent model of the other values. In Japan, it seems, one is forever trying to guess what the other person is thinking in order to avoid a direct clash of ideas or wishes. You rarely hear the equivalent of an American *no* in Japan; one student has catalogued some sixteen different ways of avoiding a direct *no*, because that nasty word marks a break of harmony.[1] In Japan, you almost never hear an argument. Disagreements are almost always expressed indirectly, as if

---

[1] Keiko Ueda, "Sixteen Ways to Avoid Saying 'No' in Japanese," in *Intercultural Encounters with Japan*, eds. John Condon and Mitsuko Saito (Tokyo: Simul Press, 1974), pp. 185–192.

talking in a code even though each party knows there is a clear conflict. Confrontation, the medium of major social change in the United States today, appears almost only between groups or factions (as with the many factions of leftist student groups), not between individuals; and even between these groups there tends to be ritual quality to the confrontation.

Japan has an unusual history. For thousands of years it was isolated from the rest of the world, never invaded or occupied by foreigners until the end of World War II, and organized in a vertical structure something like medieval Europe. Even today, old people are regarded as superior to the young, and the male is treated as superior to the female. There are similar, clear-cut rankings that govern all aspects of the social order from how one speaks to another to where one sits in a Japanese room. I mention Japan here because it provides such a sharp contrast to values and communication patterns in the United States. And this illustration points out that an ethical principle of communication that serves one society may not serve another. As noted, however, the value of maintaining harmony is not alien to the United States. Nor are feelings of individualism totally absent in Japan. The question is when there is a conflict between the two values, which do we encourage?

Over many hundreds of years, the Japanese evolved one means of dealing with this kind of conflict. This is expressed in the terms *honne* and *tatemae*. *Honne* means one's true voice, what one really feels; *tatemae* means, literally, the outer structure of a building, and thus is what one is socially obliged to say or do. For most Americans, I suspect, this sounds like making a virtue of hypocrisy—thinking one thing and saying the opposite. For the Japanese, however—particularly those who are older—it is a practical resolution to an otherwise irreconcilable problem. In practice it also seems to require more time to discuss a subject in Japanese than it would in American English. This is because one must proceed cautiously in Japan, giving clues and hints about one's thoughts and trying to decipher those of the other party. The system also is maintained through a greater frequency of middlemen and go-betweens, who help to interpret for one party what the other wishes or is thinking. This, too, is counter to American preferences for individualism, but it also helps to promote a sense of interdependence and elaborate obligations to those who have helped or been helped in the past.

In summary, what one ought to say or not say depends in part on values of the society. We may assume, however, that in every society there will be conflicts when a person thinks one thing, but feels constrained to say something else in order not to disrupt things. If we project the ethics of individualism, we can run the risk of what some conservative philosophers call fragmentation, a kind of centrifugal force, which might scatter the individuals in all directions. Thus the fear of many conservatives is of anarchy, no structure whatsoever. On the other hand, if we project the values of maintaining social harmony, we run the risk of what some more liberal critics view as a closed system, one that exists to maintain the status quo, a centripetal force that sacrifices the individual in the name of order.

If you will recall the conversation between the officer's wives, you will note a simpler form of this conflict within our own society. Were this situation to occur in Japan, I suspect the junior officer's wife (if she would have called at all) would first have done some detective work to find out if the invitation would be accepted and probably would have indirectly alerted the other officer's wife that she would be calling. And even if this had gone awry, the wife offering the invitation would have recognized the refusal much sooner and not persevered to the brutal end. Had such a conversation actually occurred in Japan, which seems unlikely, most Japanese, I suspect, would criticize both women—the younger for her stupidity, the older for her emotionalism. In the United States, there may be supporters for each of the wives, for each in her own way was an individual candidly speaking her mind. (Each of you, individually, can decide what you would have—should have—done in such a situation.)

Fidelity

Related to the earlier issue of candor is a somewhat less subjective issue that we might call fidelity. A high fidelity (hi-fi) record and record player are those that claim to most faithfully reproduce the actual sounds of the music as originally performed. Hi-fi today is a chiché, but when the term came into vogue in the late 1950s, it served to distinguish the older records (the old 78 r.p.m. records), which were scratchy and in the older phonographs put forth a limited range of sounds, from the new ones. Martin Maloney has pointed out that one feature of those early record jackets was to bring considerable attention to the technical side of the recording itself; that is, the music might be lousy and the band or orchestra second-rate, but if the recording sounded realistic because of a superior recording technique, that was reason enough to buy it.

Those in the more technical side of information transmission— communications—hold to a comparable ethical principle. That is, the closer the message received is to the message sent, the better. The message may be true or false, may lead to war or lead to peace, but the first responsibility in communication is to get that message through with a minimum of loss and distortion. We must say minimum, of course, because in theory (and practice) there is always some loss and some distortion. At the very best, a message received can only be the same as transmitted, it can never be more or better than that.

There are several means of facilitating the accurate reception of a message sent. One of the most familiar is simple redundancy. If we value fidelity, we must then also allow or perhaps encourage redundancy in some forms. In conversations, as we have noted, our behavior is highly redundant—our words, our inflection and tone of voice, our facial expressions, posture, gestures, and so on. If we restrict many of these forms, we lessen the chances for the message coming across; and if fidelity is a good thing, then we must be careful about being impatient with redundancy.

Still more important, perhaps, is feedback. In interpersonal communication feedback usually means some acknowledgment from the listener to the person who conveyed the message. As we noted before this is often a matter of course, such as repeating a specific message we have been given over the phone. (That we may tend to do this more when we must pass on the message to another party than when the message is directed to us is interesting in itself. It suggests that we are more conscious of fidelity when we are responsible as a conduit or channel than when we are the person spoken to directly.) While it may be that our feedback is implied in our response, it is still curious. At any rate, if fidelity of communication is to be encouraged, it would seem to be unethical to discourage or prevent such feedback. In this sense, a person of power who cuts off reactions to his or her communication (such as the president refusing to read certain newspapers or watch certain television reports) has acted not just foolishly or defensively, but unethically as well. In other words, it is not fair to cut off anyone, including oneself, from knowing if a message received is sufficiently close to the message sent. This idea probably seems more familiar in the form of allowing questions, criticism, and suggestions from the audience, students, employees, readers, electorate, and all those in a lesser position of power. I suspect, however, that this encouragement often has more to do with providing a possible catharsis for those who have been talked to than as an ethical responsibility for both sender and receiver.

We might state this idea in stronger, clearer terms; it is wrong to ever express something to somebody without determining, as best one can, whether what was understood was what was intended. If so, then maybe most authority figures—parents, teachers, and administrators— are frequently ethically irresponsible.

This ethical principle, however, is not without its problems, for it too can clash with other principles, including the two we have already considered. Suppose one is told to report to others something that one believes or knows is false. In the interest of candor should one refuse to do so, or do so but add one's own opinion? Or suppose one is asked to convey a message that is sure to cause commotion or severely hurt another's feelings? Should one report the message as given, or may one alter it somewhat (clean it up or say it better) in order to reduce friction? This is a familiar problem, not an abstract matter of ethics. In some cases the reason may be simple personal self-interest, "He'll kill me if I tell him that!" In some cases it may be concern for the other that motivates changing the message, "She'll die if I tell her that!" In either case, I suspect that the usual reaction is to place other values above that of fidelity of transmission. But at the same time, I suspect that most people would hold to the ethics of faithful transmission as a basic ethical responsibility.

Some persons earn their living largely through managing that difficult balancing act. Across cultures, for example, interpreters are hired to translate faithfully what they are told in one language into an appropriate form in another. But they know that some things cannot be directly translated and also that sometimes a person mistakenly says one thing but means another. They must judge when and how to modify what is said in their translation. Usually they are not praised when they do their job well; they were just doing their job, after all. But if they misguess and alter the message the way they think it was probably meant or adapt it to the recipient's language and culture, they may be criticized as arrogant or incompetent. Spokesmen for officials, such as the presidential news secretary, must similarly judge when and how to alter what he knows to fit the occasion. Perhaps the more impersonal the messenger, the easier is the task to present messages faithfully.

Deception

In a laissez-faire system of marketing, the seller gets away with whatever he can. If he oversteps his bounds and offends enough customers, he will go out of business. The burden is thus primarily on the consumer, the watchword is *caveat emptor*—let the buyer beware. In recent years in the United States, many laws have been established to govern advertising and product marketing; false advertising, misleading or incomplete package labeling, and so on can be punished by law.

We seem to put our mouth where our money is. Advertising and labeling laws are devised to protect the consumer and to prevent deceit that causes financial loss. But outside of the commercial world, we have—fortunately, I believe—no laws governing honesty. We can say anything we want. We can exaggerate, conceal information, or tell outlandish lies, usually without any legal responsibility. *Caveat auditor*—let the listener beware. There is an assumption that most habitual deceivers will be caught up with and socially punished through the alienation of others.

But do we hold any general ethical principles about conscious distortions? Some might say that exaggerating is often quite harmless and even sometimes a source of pleasure. After all, we can recognize most exaggeration or soon learn to identify people who always seem to exaggerate about personal problems, gripes, or achievements. But what of a person who exaggerates, say, the marital problems of a neighbor? If we were the neighbor, we might not be so tolerant.

What of withholding information—not telling an employer or a prospective mate about a shady past, criminal record, drug or drinking problem, or a previous marriage? Is it not each person's right to say or not say what he wishes? In a court we must take an oath to tell the truth, the whole truth, and nothing but the truth. We demand no oaths from one another, fortunately, but as an ethical principle do we have any comparable expectations?

In such cases, and we could add many more, we might want to say, "It all depends." But the issue raised here is whether each of us really does have some general principle that is revealed in our behavior and that disturbs us when we violate it, much as we might have a general principle about more obvious ethical issues.

Acknowledgment

Very closely related to the previous issue is one that might seem simpler still. This may be regarded as minimal feedback, or simply acknowledgment. To indicate that you are listening to a person, whether or not you show that you have understood what was said, would be the simplest example. Is it ethical to appear to ignore what is being said to you? Perhaps you would say, no, of course not. What, then, of letting a telephone ring without answering it? I am told that some people cannot bear to let a phone ring without answering the phone, but I can and do, and I know that others can also. But some friends say that is irresponsible. Is it proper to let a message sent go unreceived? And although still further from interpersonal communication as we have been discussing it in this book, what of receiving a letter and not reading it, or receiving it, reading it, but not replying that you have received it. Is that responsible? In some respects the failure to acknowledge a letter received is more unethical than not answering a telephone, because the letter at least identifies the sender, whereas the phone ringing does not.

One may argue that it depends on who is expressing a message and what kind of message is being expressed. To not reply to a friend's letter is to be discouraged, but to not reply to unsolicited advertising is another matter. All right, but what then of a letter that begins, "You don't know me, but . . . "? Or, if you will allow unsolicited mail advertising to go unacknowledged, then what of an unsolicited telephone advertising campaign or a visit by a door-to-door salesman? Is there any obligation to listen at all? If you see a salesman coming to your door, is it ethical to go to the door and tell the salesperson that you don't want to buy anything, or to hide and pretend you are not home?

These questions may seem tedious or trivial, but there seems to be an ethical issue here of considerable, probably increasing, importance. Today we are surfeited with information that we care little about and some of which we may find offensive.

Consistency of Word and Act

It is not difficult to make a virtue of consistency. As we have noted throughout this book, without certain consistencies there could be no language, no meaning, and no communication. To perceive any pattern, whether it is in grammar, or semantics, or any aspect of interpersonal communication, assumes a large measure of consistency. Were this our only concern about consistency, there might be no need to speak of this as an ethical issue. But what of other inconsistencies that confuse communication?

There are inconsistencies between what one says and how one says it, and between what one says and what one does. Perhaps most of us notice inconsistent behavior in others more readily than in our own behavior. What of the person who says, "Let's get together some time, any time," but who makes no effort to meet the person he encouraged and who seems to rebuff any such attempt on the part of the other? If communication includes all behavior, then it seems this person is expressing an inconsistent message. Shall we ignore this because some people are that way, or we're all that way sometimes? Or might we judge this to be an unfair communication, which confuses and maybe hurts the other party who expected sincerity—i.e., consistency between words and actions? What of the parent who scolds the child for lying, and then in the next moment when the phone rings tells the child, "Answer it and if it is for me, tell them I'm not here." Why is it that we may have stronger feelings about the vice of lying than the virtue of consistency?

It is interesting that within the realm of professional role behavior, we do not easily excuse such inconsistencies. If we board a bus to go north and the driver takes us south, or if we make a dental appointment for Thursday and arrive to find that the dentist has taken a day off, we do not readily shrug this off. Perhaps it is because we have specific expectations.

What seems ethically irresponsible in some examples of inconsistency between words and other behaviors that communicate is that the perceiver of such conflicts is left confused and irritated. If he follows what the actions seem to indicate, he may later be chided for not following the words; but if he tries to follow what the words indicate, he may be frustrated by the actions that prevent this. We have already mentioned examples of persons labeled as mentally disturbed who seem to seek to protect themselves through paradoxical speech ("Don't believe anything I tell you. I always lie."),[2] and we noted Berne's book, *Games People Play*, which considers such inconsistencies as basic rules of the game. But it misses the point simply to call such behavior sick, neurotic, or crazy, when such inconsistencies are so readily apparent around us and sometimes in our own behavior. Hence this ethical issue can be seen as a middle ground between a "that's life" attitude and a "that's sick" judgment.

In short, if we have feelings that it is generally not right to deceive another person by telling a deliberate falsehood, we might also feel that it is not right to deliberately contradict our words with inconsistent actions. So far as I know, we have no good word in English that quite expresses this judgment. Hypocrisy is not quite the same, and inconsistency seems too general and bland. Perhaps only the relatively recent acknowledgment that communication includes much more than words has made this a significant issue.

To complicate things a little further, let's assume that a person contradicts words and actions in the interests of compromising the values of candor and social harmony. This seems to be a plausible rationalization in many cases. That is, suppose a person to whom you don't want to talk calls on you. In the interest of avoiding hurt feelings, your words say that you welcome your visitor, "Well, hello there. How good to see you!" At almost the same time, however, you

[2] Paul Watzlawick, et al., *Pragmatics of Human Communication* (New York: W. W. Norton, 1967), pp. 187–253.

stand up, put on your coat, and make other motions that indicate you were just leaving—hoping the visitor will take the hint. Some may feel this is the natural thing to do or at least an ethically preferable alternative to either violating your own feelings by actually welcoming the visitor, or hurting the visitor's feelings by saying you don't want to talk to him or her. (If you suggest just saying you were about to go out, or asking the visitor to come back some other time, I don't see that these are really very different from the word-action ruse.) Anyway, what's wrong with this? For one thing, you may smugly put the hapless visitor into a double bind. If he or she takes the hint from your actions, you may tell yourself, "Well, I didn't tell the visitor to go—that's his (or her) problem." And if the visitor doesn't take the hint, you may mentally accuse him or her of being insensitive! In short, you give yourself two rationalized options and your visitor none. That seems unfair.

Keeping Confidences and Sharing

Maybe this belongs in our dialectic bag. At every level from the most personal to official government there are strong ethical (sometimes legal) feelings about keeping confidences or maintaining a promised secrecy. Simply stated one might say that it is wrong to tell somebody something that you have promised to keep secret. The dialectical principle is that for something to be a secret, it must be something that has been shared already. In short, "I will tell you if you promise not to tell anybody else." And if you do tell somebody else, the more grievous sin is not in having let the secret out, but in having betrayed a trust. And yet, to relate this to our previous discussion, many secrets are told with the expectation that they will be told again. The tag line of a rumor is more often, "don't tell anybody," than "pass it on." But the effect is the same.

One problem with keeping a confidence, as most grade school children will tell you, is that it makes an impossible demand to be loyal to the person who told you the secret at the expense of loyalty to some other friend who is never to be told. Moreover, once the word is out that a secret exists (I know something you don't know), the poor recipient of the secret news may be badgered to tell if he or she knows the secret and then, if he or she admits that much, to tell the secret itself. Goffman touches on this when he writes of "dark secrets" and the importance of keeping secret that there is a secret—which neither grade school kids nor the CIA manage very well, and a kind of opposite, the secret that there is no secret—which the Wizard of Oz did not manage very well.

At any rate, secrecy and sharing involve loyalties and identification. If I tell you a secret and make you promise not to tell anybody else, I am demanding your loyalty and identification with me, or my team, or my (our) company, nation, and so on. So we might begin with the question, "Is it ethical to encourage another person to hear a secret with the promise that the person never tell?" More generally, are all purveyors of secrets not very far removed from those who would spread rumor and gossip?

Before answering, note that there are some professionals who not only are respected listeners of secrets, but are also committed to maintaining those secrets. Clergymen, particularly—the image is of the priest in the confessional box—are the most notable. But medical doctors, lawyers, and news reporters maintaining their sources of information are not very different. Then there are secret societies that use arcane rituals, passwords, or oaths of loyalty—the Mafia, the K.K.K., fraternal organizations, the Masons, Greek societies on campus, and so on. In such societies maintaining secrecy is the test of and guarantee of loyalty to an identification with those in the group.

Our cultural values are largely opposed to the secrecy of secret societies. There is something too exclusive and divisive, too undemocratic, about them. If the secret society is admired, it is usually for good works or novelty (such as Shriners' hospitals and parades) rather than for their mystery. Significantly, most of these secret societies adhere to a vertical hierarchy of rankings and a pervasive set of complementary relationships within the organization. (All of the groups mentioned above do, I believe, clearly divide men and women within the organization if both sexes are admitted.)

Perhaps it is wise to separate secrets of initiation from more casual secrets of the gossipy kind. The former may be of little or no interest to other people in general—indeed, may be meaningless—whereas the latter are often about other people. So considering only the nonorganizational secrets, one ethical issue that we have already mentioned immediately reappears; the subject of the gossip has no means to refute or correct the secret information. This is the odious quality of rumor, and the very reason rumors usually go unchecked. Moreover, if a rumor surfaces and the subject hears of it, he or she is faced with another dilemma of the kind discussed earlier—a double bind, whether to publicly deny a rumor and run the risk of further disseminating the gossip, or to say nothing and seemingly confirm the rumor.

There are other reasons to object to keeping certain kinds of secrets. Norbert Wiener in *The Human Use of Human Beings*, assailed the practice of keeping scientific secrets, "classified information." [3] On practical, theoretical and ethical grounds as well, he argued that information that is kept secret is no longer information. Information by definition must be shared. He compared the stockpiling of secrets with the stockpiling of weapons, which become obsolete long before they rust. As a scientist (who himself contributed much to weaponry, as well as cybernetic theory and technology), he knew that there was never much difference in the information and capabilities of scientists and technicians in different nations, and that no nation any more than any individual could claim to have created or discovered or invented anything. All developments or advancements rested on the work of others. In short, the spirit of science is the spirit, the necessity, of sharing; secrecy is its antithesis, even its nemesis. The implication is that for a scientist to withhold a secret would be to violate a trust of the scientific community.

To the extent that a doctor is a member of a scientific community, his case should not be very different. But to withhold a personal or interpersonal secret is another matter. If a doctor discovers that his patient has cancer, should he tell the patient? Should he tell the patient's husband or wife? Should he inform the patient's employer? Suppose a doctor is a close, personal friend of a young couple and he makes this unfortunate prognosis—incurable cancer. One supposes the doctor would tell either the husband or wife, but which one? And if he tells the wife or the husband, and that person asks him not to tell the other, then what? If a priest knows that the person who confesses has done and may again do harm to others, what are the priest's obligations and

[3] Norbert Wiener, *The Human Use of Human Beings: Cybernetics and Society*, 2nd Rev. ed. (Garden City: Doubleday Anchor, 1954), ch. 7.

loyalties? Assume the priest gives advice that he learns was not heeded? When, if ever, may he betray this trust? A journalist receives information from a person who is declared a criminal. The information might lead to the apprehension of that person and possibly the prevention of some future criminal act. In terms of professional survival, he knows that any breach of trust threatens both his own survival and that of many other journalists, who, ironically, do much to expose gossip and innuendo and thus prevent much secrecy. What to do? Such are real and personal issues that are resolved in various ways according to each person's ethical judgments. Descriptions of interpersonal communication or communication theory alone will not yield the ethical principles, but the actions based on ethical principles may alter the acts of interpersonal communication.

Access to Secrets and Invasions of Privacy

Every year thousands of teachers write letters of recommendation for students who wish to be admitted to colleges. Until recently, such letters were supposed to be strictly confidential—between the writer of the letter and the appropriate authorities, who were to decide to admit or refuse admission to the candidate. The student, about whom the letter was written, was not allowed to see the letter. The advantage of this system was that the writer could be more frank, not having to worry about any reaction from the student. The disadvantage of this was that misinformation, either willful on the part of some spiteful teacher or well-intended but erroneous, could go into the student's file and influence the student's future prospects. A law was passed recently that altered this system, giving the student the right to have access to what was said about him or her. The details of that law need not concern us; the ethical issue, however, surely does. As a general principle we can ask, is it ethical for any organization or institution to maintain information about a person that the person cannot have access to?

Millions of Americans today are on file in a variety of organizations and governmental agencies without having access to those files, without being able to correct misinformation or refute allegations. Computer technology has aided bureaucracies in compiling and combining assorted information—tax forms, credit accounts, employment and social security records, and so on. More ominous are reports compiled by the covert organizations, such as the FBI and detective agencies. Our purpose here is neither to increase the national level of paranoia, nor to concentrate on governmental files. It is simply the more general question of a person's right to know what is said or written about that person.

In daily interpersonal activities, is it proper to say things about one person to other people that one would not also say to that person? And, we might also ask, is it fair for a person to ask another what has been said about him or her? We may believe that anybody who worries too much about what other people are saying has more than an ethical problem to contend with. And yet the familiar setting of the small town where everybody seems to know everything about everybody, which creates an atmosphere of uneasiness, is one that is often judged unethical. The problem with gossip, as we suggested previously, is not so much that information of a sort is being spread, but rather that the information is passed along in secret.

Closely related to the question of access to information about oneself is the question of privacy. There has been considerable concern in recent years about the invasion of privacy. Most popular attention has been directed to electronic eavesdropping, the bugging of a meeting place or bedroom, wire-taps on telephones, and so on. The debate has largely been cast between the individual's rights of privacy and security for a larger public.

In the spring of 1975 Jay Gourley, a young reporter for the *National Enquirer*, created a news event by hauling off the trash from the home of Henry Kissinger. He then sorted through the trash to see what he could find of interest. Legally, there was no way of stopping Gourley or anybody else who wants to take away a person's trash. But the ethical issue of an invasion of privacy disturbed many, including fellow journalists. Legal issues aside, to what extent is it ethical to intrude on the personal matters of another? If I throw away a letter, do you have the right to read it?

For social scientists, too, this is an ethical issue; in recent years some guidelines have been suggested for some kinds of inquiries. But as a teacher of communication I have an uneasy conscience when I ask students to go and observe communication behavior, which is public, if the people involved are not aware of being studied. Of course, if a researcher were to always tell people that he was undertaking a certain study and request their permission to be observed, his results might be of little value because we can assume that the subjects' behavior would be altered by their awareness of being observed. Hence the dilemma for the field worker. Participant observation techniques—in which the researcher joins a group as if a member but actually to study that group—involve a double problem, of course. Not only does the researcher observe their behavior without their consent, but the researcher may also have been admitted to the group through deception.

Justifications for such behavior are many: in the pursuit of knowledge and thus for the greater good; just doing what I was assigned to do; all information will be kept confidential and names will be disguised, so nobody is harmed; and so on. But the pursuit of knowledge may sometimes be a euphemism for getting a degree or publishing a paper that will lead to personal advancement, and to say that nobody will be harmed is fatuous. Who knows?

Some might invoke here and elsewhere the Golden Rule or some version of it—I wouldn't mind if somebody studied me without my knowledge, so it should be all right if I study somebody else without their knowing. But one problem with this is that it imposes one's own ethical standards on others without finding out how the others feel.

Other Issues

There has been no attempt to exhaust the possible ethical issues that arise in interpersonal communication; I am not even sure that those presented here are the most common or the most important issues. For example, we could have considered as Wiener has, the issue of blocking or jamming the communication of others; whereas Wiener was more concerned with mass media jamming—garbling radio signals and the like—to prevent reception, we might consider the more subtle and familiar kinds of blocking—cutting off a person before he or she has made the point, changing the subject when one knows the other person wants to talk more, or nonverbally acting in ways that are intended to distract another from what that person wants to express. Or, echoing Confucius, we might inquire about the ethics of talking too much, or worse, sensing that the other party wishes we would stop talking, ask about it in such a way that the other person may feel obliged to say, "No, go on, it's interesting." Or what of the ploys of choosing the occasion to inquire about something or ask a special favor when the person asked is most constrained to agree. For many, I suppose, this is what human relations are all about. And yet many would disapprove of, say, funeral directors who take advantage of the mourner's mental state to sell his most expensive merchandise, or ambulance chasers, or the Iagos in our midst who prey upon the vulnerable's fears and suspicions.

We may argue any of these issues in two ways: (1) that there can be no absolute ethical standard; but also (2) that you have to draw the line somewhere—some behaviors are harmless, some merely annoying or impolite, but some downright unethical. This is more or less what some of the defendants in the Watergate case attempted—distinguishing among "dirty tricks," "political hardball," and simply "illegal." But as in that celebrated case, which now seems more a matter of assessing ethical standards than simply dividing the legal from the illegal, each person will draw the line at a different spot. It all depends. We must think of that. We must also think of what else will depend on our choice and action.

Ethics and Models

Earlier in the book we mentioned three of the most frequently used models, or metaphors, for giving shape to the process of interpersonal communication—as a drama, as a game, as a computer processing of information. If one is able to state preferences—or at least advantages—in viewing communication as if it were one of these more than the others, then the ethical implications of such a choice should also be considered. Our model will greatly influence our ethical standards. If any metaphor seems more abstract than our own daily behavior, then it might be appropriate to say that our ethics will influence our preference among models.

Suppose, for example, one is impressed by the cybernetic vision of interpersonal communication. Communication is a very elaborate process of sending, receiving, processing, and resending bits of information. If so, it would seem that the ethics of fidelity and consistency come to the fore. The good computer does what it is programmed to do; it does not distort its calculations to make another computer happy, it does not assert its own will—it has none. All information should be public; computers keep no secrets. It is always alert and responsive; it does not pretend to be turned off when it is really on.

But if communication is more like a game than like the efficient transmission and processing of information, then we may have other ethical standards. Anything goes—within the rules. The important thing is to win, however that is defined in the particular game. If the person one is talking to is, as viewed in a game model, an opponent, then unless there is an ethical aspect to the rules themselves, one may do or say anything in order to win. The ethics toward others on the same team, however, should be different. Among fellow team members secrecy is permitted or encouraged, both candor and harmony required, and consistency, too—to be a good team player. Toward the opponents—whatever one can get away with. I remain intrigued by the popularity of the game metaphor in the United States in recent years, and I have wondered if part of the appeal arises from or at least goes along with a widespread cynicism and the appeal of the anti-hero, the proliferation of identification groups into "we" and "they" divisions—the men/women game, the younger/older game, the black/white game, and so on. Perhaps the payoff of cynicism is more cynicism.

The dramatic model seems to have yet another combination of ethical themes. If there are clearly cast roles, each of these may follow to a great extent its own ethical standard—the self-assertive player, the harmonizer, the one from whom secrets are kept, and maybe the ambiguous concept of an audience from whom no secrets are kept—except for the secret that they are part of the drama, too. Each role with its consistent behavior and ethic, which makes that behavior consistent, clarifies the heroes, heroines, villains, and bit players. Some all-embracing ethic determines the kind of drama—a comedy of manners, perhaps, or a Greek tragedy where the information that was kept secret from all but the audience is revealed in the end—the truth-must-out ethic. Still, harmony among the players seems a dominant theme, for if anybody muffs a line or acts out of character, the others must cover for the poor player so that the show can go on.

These are somewhat fanciful applications of ethics and models, but the intention is quite serious. No attempt to describe what we feel interpersonal communication *is* can be fully separated from what we feel interpersonal communication *ought to be.*

RECOMMENDED
BOOKS

Argyle, Michael, ed. *Social Encounters. Readings in Social Interaction.* Middlesex, England and Baltimore: Penguin Books, 1973.

―――. *The Psychology of Interpersonal Behavior.* 2nd ed. Middlesex, England and Baltimore: Penguin Books, 1972.

―――. *Social Interaction.* New York: Atherton Press, 1969.

Aristotle. *The Rhetoric.* Edited and Translated by Lane Cooper. New York: Appleton Century, Crofts, 1932, 1960.

Bales, Robert F. *Interaction Process Analysis.* Cambridge: Addison-Wesley, 1950.

―――. *Personality and Interpersonal Behavior.* New York: Holt, Rinehart and Winston, 1970.

Barnlund, Dean C. *Interpersonal Communication: Survey and Studies.* Boston: Houghton Mifflin, 1968.

Bateson, Gregory. *Steps to an Ecology of Mind.* San Francisco: Chandler Publishing Co., 1972.

Berelson, Bernard, and Gary Steiner. *Human Behavior: An Inventory of Scientific Findings.* New York: Harcourt Brace Jovanovich, 1964.

Berlo, David K. *The Process of Communication.* New York: Holt, Rinehart and Winston, 1960.

Birdwhistell, Ray L. *Kinesics and Context*. Philadelphia: University of Pennsylvania Press, 1970.

Black, Max, *Models and Metaphors: Studies in Language and Philosophy*. Ithaca: Cornell University Press, 1962.

Boulding, Kenneth. *The Image*. Ann Arbor: Ann Arbor Paperbacks, 1961.

Brown, Roger. *Words and Things*. New York: The Free Press, 1959, 1966.

————. *Social Psychology*. New York: Free Press, 1965.

Bryson, Lyman. *The Communication of Ideas*. New York: Institute for Religious and Social Studies, 1947.

Burke, Kenneth. *A Grammar of Motives*. New York: Prentice-Hall, 1945.

————. *A Rhetoric of Motives*. New York: Prentice-Hall, 1950.

Carpenter, Edmund and Marshall McLuhan, eds. *Explorations in Communication*. Boston: Beacon Press, 1960.

Carroll, J. G., ed. *Language, Thought and Reality: Selected Writings of Benjamin Lee Whorf*. New York: John Wiley and Sons, 1956.

Cherry, Colin. *On Human Communication*. Cambridge: Technology Press of MIT, 1957, 1966.

Condon, John C. *Semantics and Communications*. 2nd ed. New York: Macmillan, 1975.

————, and Fathi Yousef, *An Introduction to Intercultural Communication*. Indianapolis: Bobbs-Merrill, 1975.

Dance, Frank, ed. *Human Communication Theory*. New York: Holt, Rinehart and Winston, 1967.

Davitz, J. R. *The Communication of Emotional Meaning*. New York: McGraw-Hill, 1964.

Deutsch, Morton, and Robert Krauss. *Theories in Social Psychology*. New York: Basic Books, Inc., 1965.

Duncan, Hugh D. *Symbols in Society*. New York: Oxford University Press, 1968.

Festinger, Leon. *A Theory of Cognitive Dissonance*. New York: Row, Peterson, 1957.

Fink, Donald G. *Computers and the Human Mind*. New York: Doubleday Anchor, 1966.

Goffman, Ervin. *Behavior in Public Places*. New York: Free Press, 1963.

————. *Encounters*. Indianapolis: Bobbs-Merrill, 1961.

———. *Interaction Ritual.* New York: Doubleday Anchor, 1967.

———. *The Presentation of Self in Everyday Life.* New York: Doubleday Anchor, 1959.

Hall, Edward T. *The Hidden Dimension.* New York: Doubleday, 1966.

———. *The Silent Language.* New York: Doubleday, 1959.

Jourard, Sidney. *The Transparent Self.* New York: Van Nostrand, Reinhold Co., 1964.

Katz, Elihu, and Paul Lazarsfeld. *Personal Influence.* New York: The Free Press, 1955.

Homans, George. *The Human Group.* New York: Harcourt Brace Jovanovich, 1950.

Knapp, Mark L. *Nonverbal Communication in Human Interaction.* New York: Holt, Rinehart and Winston, 1972.

Labov, William. *The Social Stratification of English in New York City.* Berkeley: Center for Applied Linguistics, 1966.

Laing, R. D. *Self and Others.* London: Tavistock Publications, 1961.

Langer, Susanne. *Philosophy in a New Key.* Cambridge: Harvard University Press, 1942.

Lee, Dorothy. *Freedom and Culture.* Englewood Cliffs: Prentice-Hall, 1959.

Laver, John, and Sandy Hutcheson, eds. *Communication in Face to Face Interaction.* Middlesex, England and Baltimore: Penguin Books, 1972.

Matson, Floyd, and Ashley Montague, eds. *The Human Dialogue: Perspectives on Communication.* New York: Free Press, 1967.

Mead, George H. *Mind, Self and Society.* Chicago: University of Chicago Press, 1934.

Mehrabian, Albert. *Silent Messages.* Belmont, Calif.: Wadsworth Publishing Co., 1971.

Miller, George. *Language and Communication.* New York: McGraw-Hill, 1951.

Morris, Charles. *Signs, Language and Behavior.* New York: Prentice-Hall, 1946.

Newcomb, Theodore. *The Acquaintance Process.* New York: Holt, Rinehart and Winston, 1961.

Pittenger, R. E., C. F. Hockett, and J. J. Danehy. *The First Five Minutes.* New York: Martineau, 1960.

Rapoport, Anatol. *Fights, Games and Debates*. New York: Harper and Row, 1960.

Rogers, Carl. *Counseling and Psychotherapy*. Boston: Houghton Mifflin, 1942.

————. *On Becoming a Person*. Boston: Houghton Mifflin, 1961.

Ruesch, Jurgen. *Therapeutic Communication*. New York: W. W. Norton, 1961.

————, and Gregory Bateson. *Communication: Social Matrix of Psychiatry*. New York: W. W. Norton, 1951.

————, and Weldon Kees. *Nonverbal Communication*. Berkeley: University of California Press, 1956.

Satir, Virginia. *Conjoint Family Therapy*. rev. ed. Palo Alto: Science and Behavior Books, 1967.

Shannon, Clyde, and Warren Weaver. *The Mathematical Theory of Communication*. Urbana: University of Illinois Press, 1951.

Smith, Alfred G., ed. *Communication and Culture*. New York: Holt, Rinehart and Winston, 1966.

Smith, Arthur L. *Language, Communication and Rhetoric in Black America*. New York: Harper and Row, 1969.

Sommer, Robert. *Personal Space*. Englewood Cliffs, N.J.: Prentice-Hall, 1969.

Stewart, Edward C. *American Cultural Patterns: A Cross-Cultural Perspective*. Pittsburgh: Regional Council for International Education, 1971.

Tagiuri, Renato, and Luigi Petrullo, eds. *Person Perception and Interpersonal Behavior*. Stanford: Stanford University Press, 1958.

von Bertalanffy, Ludwig. *General Systems Theory*. New York: Braziller, 1968.

Watzlawick, Paul, Janet Beavin, and Don Jackson. *Pragmatics of Human Communication*. New York: W. W. Norton, 1967.

Wiener, Norbert. *The Human Use of Human Beings: Cybernetics and Society*. 2nd rev. ed. Garden City: Doubleday Anchor, 1954.

INDEX